THE FOCAL EASY GUIDE

DVD STUDIO PRO

G000135263

The Focal Easy Guide Series

Focal Easy Guides are the best choice to get you started with new software, whatever your level. Refreshingly simple, they do not attempt to cover everything, focusing solely on the essentials needed to get immediate results.

Ideal if you need to learn a new software package quickly, the Focal Easy Guides offer an effective, time-saving introduction to the key tools, not hundreds of pages of confusing reference material. The emphasis is on quickly getting to grips with the software in a practical and accessible way to achieve professional results.

Highly illustrated in color, explanations are short and to the point. Written by professionals in a user-friendly style, the guides assume some computer knowledge and an understanding of the general concepts in the area covered, ensuring they aren't patronizing!

Series editor: Rick Young (www.digitalproduction.net)

Director and Founding Member of the UK Final Cut User Group, Apple Solutions Expert and freelance television director/editor, Rick has worked for the BBC, Sky, ITN, CNBC, and Reuters. Also a Final Cut Pro Consultant and author of the best-selling *The Easy Guide to Final Cut Pro*.

Titles in the series:

The Easy Guide to Final Cut Pro 3, Rick Young

The Focal Easy Guide to Final Cut Pro 4, Rick Young

The Focal Easy Guide to Final Cut Express, Rick Young

The Focal Easy Guide to Maya 5, Jason Patnode

The Focal Easy Guide to Discreet combustion 3, Gary M. Davis

The Focal Easy Guide to Premiere Pro, Tim Kolb

The Focal Easy Guide to Flash MX 2004, Birgitta Hosea

THE FOCAL EASY GUIDE TO
DVD STUDIO PRO 3

For new users and professionals

RICK YOUNG

ELSEVIER

AMSTERDAM • BOSTON • HEIDELBERG • LONDON • NEW YORK • OXFORD
PARIS • SAN DIEGO • SAN FRANCISCO • SINGAPORE • SYDNEY • TOKYO
Focal Press is an imprint of Elsevier

Focal Press
An imprint of Elsevier
Linacre House, Jordan Hill, Oxford OX2 8DP
30 Corporate Drive, Burlington, MA 01803

First published 2005

Copyright © 2005, Digital Production Ltd. All rights reserved
All Photographs copyright © Digital Production Ltd.
Technical Editor, Jeff Warmouth

The right of Rick Young to be identified as the author of this work has been
asserted in accordance with the Copyright, Designs and Patents Act 1988

No part of this publication may be reproduced in any material form (including
photocopying or storing in any medium by electronic means and whether
or not transiently or incidentally to some other use of this publication) without
the written permission of the copyright holder except in accordance with the
provisions of the Copyright, Designs and Patents Act 1988 or under the terms of a
licence issued by the Copyright Licensing Agency Ltd, 90 Tottenham Court Road,
London, England W1T 4LP. Applications for the copyright holder's written permission to
reproduce any part of this publication should be addressed to the publisher

Permissions may be sought directly from Elsevier's Science and Technology Rights
Department in Oxford, UK: phone: (+44) (0) 1865 843830; fax: (+44) (0) 1865 853333;
e-mail: permissions@elsevier.co.uk. You may also complete your request on-line
via the Elsevier homepage (http://www.elsevier.com), by selecting "Customer Support"
and then "Obtaining Permissions"

British Library Cataloguing in Publication Data
A catalogue record for this book is available from the British Library

Library of Congress Cataloguing in Publication Data
A catalogue record for this book is available from the Library of Congress

ISBN   0 240 51934 5

For information on all Focal Press publications visit our website at:
www.focalpress.com

Typeset by Charon Tec. Pvt Ltd, Chennai, India
www.charontec.com
Printed and bound in Italy

Working together to grow
libraries in developing countries

www.elsevier.com | www.bookaid.org | www.sabre.org

ELSEVIER   **BOOK AID**
International   Sabre Foundation

Contents

Thank You.

Fiona
Ellen
Druman
Jeff Warmouth
Charles Roberts
Marie Hooper
Kristen and Julian
Suzy and Mike
John Pin
Jonathan Smiles

The Greatest Trick Of All...

Listen up, here's the secret to making your DVDs look like they were professionally produced.

No-one knows, or cares, what went into making the DVD.

All they see is the final result... the Menus, the Buttons and of utmost importance, the Content which makes up the disk.

The Greatest Trick of All is to make your Menus look good.

Don't get carrried away with trying to be clever.

Keep it smart, keep it moving, make it easy for the viewer to access what they want, quickly and easily...

If you can achieve this your audience will see the DVD in the same light as any commerically produced disk. And you, my friend, will have earned the title of DVD Author...

Preface

Since the beginning of time, men and women have worked to reproduce and record their surrounding environment. From cave paintings to stone carvings, papyrus, wood, paper, canvas, wax, and chemicals… every substance imaginable has been used for both artistic expression and the documentation of history and culture. Regardless of whether one uses charcoal to draw, a crystal radio to tap into the airwaves, or a pinhole camera to capture images, the quest to document and interpret creative expression has always been an artistic and technological challenge.

DVDs represent the pinnacle in a long evolution of recording technology. The quality is unsurpassed by any other medium previously available to consumers. Not only is the quality fantastic, the ability to structure the material is far more advanced than previous formats. DVDs let the user, view and listen to recorded material in both, a sophisticated and interactive way.

To make DVDs, requires vision and planning. However, this vision and planning can be simple or complex. One does not need to be led through a maze of intricately woven material for a DVD to serve its purpose. The viewer's interest, first and foremost, is in the content which is presented. The DVD medium is simply there to facilitate a way of accessing this content.

This book cuts through much of the technical knowledge and jargon, which has traditionally been associated with DVD production. The techniques described will take you to the core of what DVD production is about. In no time at all, you will be producing professional looking DVDs in an easy, efficient, and manageable way. DVD Studio Pro is the tool. Your mind, as in all artistic endeavors, is the creative instrument.

Rick Young
Producer/Director/Editor
London, UK

DVD-5 and Beyond...

The first DVDs hit the market in 1996. Back then unless you had a lot of money, there was no way in the world you would be setting up any sort of system to burn DVDs. This was strictly a professional territory.

The subject of this book is how to make DVDs using the DVD-R General format onto 4.7 GB disks. You can also use DVD-RW without problems.

Some of the newer DVD burners can also burn other formats such as DVD+R and DVD+RW. A few even do DVD-RAM as well.

By all means feel free to experiment with whatever format your DVD burner can write to.

Just be aware that the methods and workflow put forward throughout this book has been tested by myself using DVD-R general disks on an Apple Superdrive.

My prediction is that there will be no fight to the death DVD format war as there was with Beta and VHS. For the simple reason that all the competing formats are the same size and the manufacturers have developed drives capable of reading, and in many cases writing, to each of the formats.

The real area of interest is the future. The Blu-ray 27 GB disks have already been forecast well in advance and dual-layer consumer DVD writers are now available.

For the moment we stand smack-bang in the midst of a technical wave which isn't even halfway spent. Ride this wave and hold on tight. We are at the beginning of a technological leap of such magnitude; the world will never be the same again.

CHAPTER 1
BASICS

Overview of DVD Production

There is no getting away from the fact that it is important to understand the technical processes involved with DVD production to effectively work with this medium. This does not mean you need to know every single detail about the inner workings of the technology – but a general overview is essential. Just as one can drive a car without knowing how to build an engine, one can author DVDs without knowing all the technical processes that go into the production of the shiny silver disks.

A DVD does nothing but hold information. This information is embedded in the pits and grooves which make up the structure of the disk. This information is what you, the "author", arranges and orders for the viewer to access. The term author is used to describe the role of the person who puts the content together which is recorded onto the DVD.

The DVD authoring process can be broken up into five distinct processes:

Content creation – As already mentioned the person watching the DVD is primarily interested in the content which has been recorded onto the disk. This content is made up of video clips, audio, and graphics. The content is produced inside of an editing  program such as Final Cut Pro and possibly other software specific to audio creation, video compositing, and/or graphic creation.

Planning – A DVD needs to be planned in advance before it is produced. The plan can be a rough sketch or a detailed outline, however, before you begin you need to have an idea of what you are trying to achieve. A basic DVD could have the sole requirement of playing immediately once inserted into a player; alternatively a DVD could be made up of many clips, stills, and audio tracks – each which link to each other according to the options chosen by the person in charge of the remote control. Regardless of how simple or complex the DVD may be, you, as the author, must decide in advance what options will be made available to the viewer once the disk is inside the DVD player.

Preparation – This is where the technical knowledge of DVD production comes into play. For a DVD to work, the information recorded onto the disk needs to be compressed into a form known as MPG-2. MPG-2 provides a way of encoding video into a file which is small in size yet high in quality. As the author of the DVD you have many

choices about how the encoding process will take place. You can choose to encode before you author the disk or you can let the encoding take place in the background while you work. You can also choose to work with QuickTime files which have been exported from Final Cut Pro, or another editing system, and save the encoding process until the disk has been authored. There are advantages and disadvantages to each of these choices and these will be covered later on.

Authoring – Think of the authoring process as being the creative and technically challenging part of putting the DVD together. Here the look of the DVD is determined, how the various components of the disk will be made accessible to the viewer, and the overall way in which the disk is laid out. You, as the DVD author, must decide the way the content on the disk can be accessed. The decisions you make during the authoring process will determine the choices available to the viewer throughout the viewing experience.

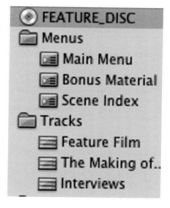

Multiplexing – This is the final stage in the production of the DVD. This is where all the elements which make up the DVD are blended together in such a way to enable set-top players to read the disk. It is similar to rendering video files inside of Final Cut Pro or burning a CD inside of an application such as Toast. Multiplexing is the last phase of producing a DVD prior to distribution.

This brief overview outlines the essential processes required to make DVDs. Not mentioned is the phase beyond authoring and multiplexing which is taking the DVD to a plant for mass replication. However, this process takes place outside

DVD Studio Pro once all the hard work of producing the DVD has taken place. Your job as the DVD author is get all the elements which make up the DVD working in a way which is simple, accessible and interesting for the intended audience. Beyond this you need to make the DVD look good – in other words, it needs to be visually appealing. There are many tools and work methods available within DVD Studio Pro to help you achieve this.

System Setup

Loading the software for DVD Studio Pro is easy to achieve and is virtually as simple as putting the supplied DVD into the DVD drive of your Mac and following the on-screen instructions. Once the software has been installed you will need to enter the serial number before you can use it.

A total of four applications are installed onto your computer:

DVD Studio Pro – for authoring DVDs.

A.Pack – used to compress audio files to AC-3 which is a compressed audio format which yields high quality files while using up very little space on the DVD.

QuickTime MPEG Encoder – this is the engine which enables you to convert your files into a form which can be read by a DVD Player.

Compressor – used for batch encoding files to MPG-2 which is the file format required for DVD production.

It is useful to locate the applications, once installed, and to place them onto the dock for convenient easy access.

DVD Studio Pro is the most important of these applications. If you wish you can comfortably ignore the others until you are experienced with DVD Studio Pro itself.

You will need a minimum of a G4 733 Mac with 256 megabytes (MB) of RAM. It is recommended you have 20 gigabytes (GB) of hard-drive space free to install the software and store the files created during the authoring process. In reality, you will need more hard-drive space than this, particularly when considering that DVD Studio Pro will most likely share your computer with Final Cut Pro which, as of version 4, is made up of five separate applications. These being: Final Cut Pro, Soundtrack, LiveType, Compressor, and Cinema tools.

At the time of writing, the most basic G4 configuration available is a G4 eMac with a 40-GB hard drive. I would suggest this would be the absolute minimum hard-drive space one should have available to effectively work with DVD Studio Pro in combination with Final Cut Pro.

It is also desirable to have more than one hard drive available. This could be in the form of an internal drive inside your Mac and an external Firewire drive. Some experts recommend that DVD Studio Pro works the best when the source files are run separate to the drive which is the home to DVD Studio Pro itself. If you only have one hard drive available then by all means work with this. Just be aware that your system may not work as efficiently as it would if two or more hard drives are available.

Other factors which will affect performance include whether your Mac is a G4 or G5 – obviously a G5 machine is better; whether you are working with a single or dual processor machine; and the amount of installed RAM.

The same rule which applies to hard disk space also applies to RAM – the more the better. . . .

Final Cut Pro and DVD Studio Pro

Final Cut Pro and DVD Studio Pro have been designed to work together. This is obvious from the look of various parts of each of the programs.

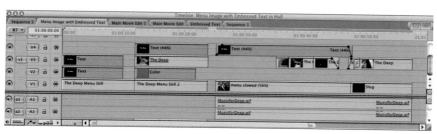

Final Cut Pro Timeline

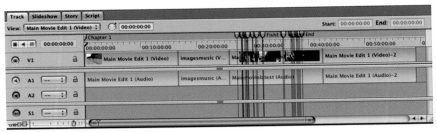

DVD Studio Pro Track Editor

Aside from the similarities with the interface the two programs compliment each other. Final Cut Pro is designed as an editing application and is well suited to producing and exporting the content which will be used inside of DVD Studio Pro. Furthermore, there is a certain level of compatibility between the two programs which has been deliberately inbuilt to make your life easier. Without jumping too far ahead, it is sufficient to say that Final Cut Pro, or even Final Cut Express, both provide ideal companion programs to assist you in producing the content needed to work with DVD Studio Pro. While it is possible to use other editing applications in combination with DVD Studio Pro, Final Cut Pro and Express are both proven and recommended.

Throughout this book I will regularly refer to Final Cut and how it can be used in combination with DVD Studio Pro.

Anatomy of a DVD

In basic terms a DVD is made up of two major components: a menu and a track. Other components which make up a DVD menu include buttons (which link to tracks or other content) a title and background image.

A track is your video that plays and a menu is a screen that lets you choose things.

Therefore, in the example titled Mountain Rescue, one can choose from two buttons. These, along with the background image and title, make up the menu.

A menu is essentially an area where you choose what you will view. Think of it like going into a restaurant and using the menu to choose your food; the difference being with a DVD you choose what you will watch. It is as simple as that!

All the components you see make up the DVD menu

Each and every menu will have a background image and at least one button. The background can be a still image or moving video. A background image which does not move is referred to as a **Still menu** while one made up of moving video is a **Motion menu**.

Buttons, as the term suggests, are areas which when pressed will activate a particular function. The "function" is determined by you – the DVD Author. Pressing a button, for example, could result in a track being played; alternatively it could link to a series of stills. A button may link from one menu to another, or perhaps take you to a clip which in turn will link to another clip.

Describing the potential of a DVD is a bit like trying to describe an emotion to a statue or colors to a blind man. The only way to get a clear understanding of these functions is to get a DVD, put it into a DVD player, and explore. You will quickly come to understand the potential and power of this medium once you have looked at several DVDs.

When creating DVDs the potential is limited by your creativity, your technical ability, and the content you have to work with. It should be clear that DVDs give you, the author, the means to present video, audio, and graphics in a flexible and creative way. How you achieve this is dependent on your ability to master the tools which DVD Studio provides you with.

As a DVD author, you will work with content made up of video, audio, graphics, and subtitles. These are referred to as **Assets**. Assets are the components you use to build the DVD.

The assets can be put together in various ways. You can independently access video and audio, thus you could, for example, instruct the DVD to play specific audio to the video clip which make up the menu background.

Stills can be ordered together in the form of **Slideshows**, with or without audio.

Subtitles can be added, optionally, at the flick of a switch on the remote control should the viewer wish to access these.

Tracks can be made to loop, thus creating a self-running DVD which will play indefinitely.

Chapter Markers can be added to tracks which effectively creates predefined markers which the viewer can jump between; very similar to jumping between chapters in a book or skipping from track to track on a record or CD.

A **Title Bar** will most often be added to each of the menus which make up the DVD; thus defining what it is the viewer is looking at before they have even touched the remote control.

Video can be added to shapes in the form of **Drop Zones** to sections within the DVD menu. This will add dimension to what would otherwise be a bland section of moving video or a still image. Just as television news and sport programs are jazzed up with fancy graphics you too can enhance your DVD with the visual techniques offered by Backgrounds, Buttons, Title Bars, and Drop Zones.

Transitions can be used when going from one menu to another, to link between a button connecting to a track, Slideshow, or another menu, or to transition from the first menu of the DVD into the main movie, for example.

Don't feel "on the outside", if these terms confuse you at this stage. If you are new to DVD authoring it will take a while to come to grips with the potential which this medium offers. You are fighting a battle on two fronts. First, you need to understand terminology which is new and unfamiliar; and you also need to understand concepts which you have likely never come across before.

Making a recording, used to be as simple as pressing "play and record", and setting the audio levels. Now you need to think beyond the two button "crash record" approach.

This is why DVDs have been called digital versatile disks. They are versatile in that the experience offered goes beyond any medium previously available – a challenge to authors in how the material is to be presented and a superior visual and audio experience for the end user.

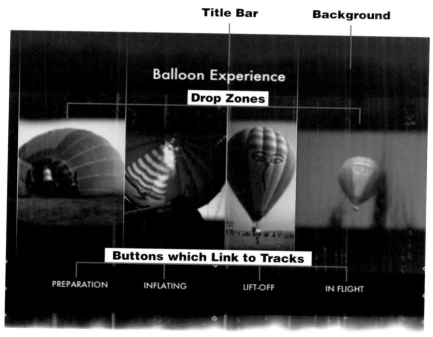

A Menu is contructed from Buttons, a Background, Drop Zones with Still or Moving Video and a Title Bar

Definition of a Professional DVD

This book aims to facilitate one single thing – to give you the knowledge needed to produce DVDs which are professional in appearance and structure. The fact that you will most likely produce DVDs on an Apple Superdrive, or external DVD burner, in a home studio set-up or office environment, will be invisible to the user. In all appearances the disks you make will look like professionally authored DVDs.

Before we move forward we need to define what exactly is a professional disk.

Professional DVDs, such as those which can be purchased or rented from commercial outlets and DVD libraries, are made up of three main components. First and the foremost is the Main Movie. In the case of a Hollywood Blockbuster the Main Movie would be the reason, in most cases, why one purchases the disk. Simply put – the Main Movie is the feature film or program which is the reason why the DVD has been created. It is the selling point for the DVD.

In addition to the Main Movie one is usually offered a Scene Index. This refers to a way of accessing various parts of the Main Movie at the press of a button. The Scene Index is accessed on a menu or several menus specific to this function. Usually scenes are accessed by buttons which will then take you to the exact point you have chosen.

Beyond the Main Movie and the Scene Index one is often presented with Additional Material. This Additional Material may be "The Making of..." the Main Movie, cast biographies, movie trailers and documentary material.

While it isn't necessary that every one of these options be offered for every single professional disk on the market, this formula – Main Movie, Additional Material, and Scene Index – is used most often for commercial DVD releases. Just look at any Hollywood produced DVD and you will see this structure forms the basis of most DVDs on the market.

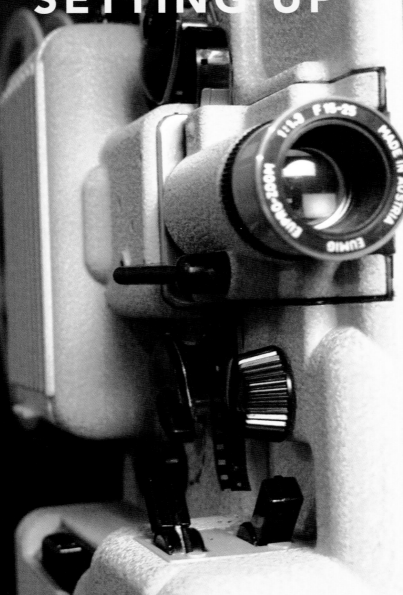

CHAPTER 2
SETTING UP

Initial Setup

If you have just opened DVD Studio Pro for the first time you will be given the choice of selecting the mode in which you wish to work.

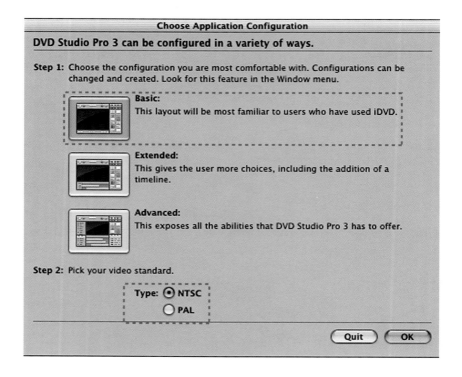

Select Basic for the moment, as this is the easiest mode to get started with. You also need to select the video standard you are working with. If you are in the USA, Canada, or Japan you need to set the video standard to NTSC. If you are in Europe, Australia, or much of Asia then PAL is the dominant format.

If you need to manually set the layout mode this can be easily achieved:

1   Choose the Window menu at the top of screen and scroll to Configurations.

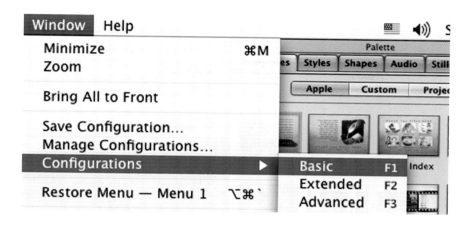

2   Choose the layout mode you wish to work with – in this case Basic. The interface will now assume the Basic configuration.

Setting Preferences

Most of the preferences can be left at their default, however, it is essential to set a few important preferences before you begin.

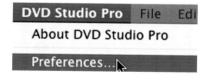

To open Preferences click on the DVD Studio Pro menu located top left of screen and scroll to Preferences.

1   Choose the DVD Studio Pro menu at the top left of screen.

2   Scroll to Preferences and release your mouse.

A window will now open giving you access to the preferences which you can customize.

The last three preferences, Encoding, Destinations and Simulator, need to be investigated. **Encoding** refers to the way in which DVD Studio Pro will process the video files to MPG-2 while **Destinations** refers to where the encoded files will be stored. The **Simulator** is used to check the DVD is working as you planned.

Destinations

Setting Destinations is similar to setting the Scratch Disks in Final Cut Pro. When files are converted to MPG-2 it is important that you instruct DVD Studio Pro where you want these files to be stored. You have several options:

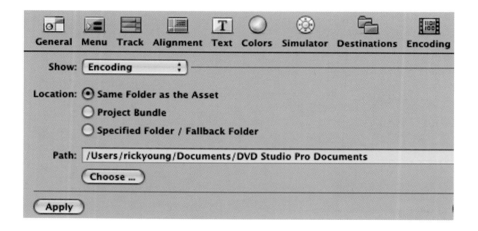

(i) Same Folder as the Asset – Assets refer to source files used by DVD Studio Pro to make up the content of the DVD. When these files are converted to MPG-2, the MPG-2 files will be stored in the same place as the original source file. This is the method I use. The advantage is that wherever your original assets are located will be the same folder as the encoded MPG-2 files. Using this method, DVD Studio Pro creates a folder titled MPG in the same location as your source files and it is here where the encoded files will be stored. I suggest

you to use this option, however, be aware that it is advisable to group your source files (assets) into a location which you choose prior to importing the assets into DVD Studio Pro. Otherwise you will end up with MPG folders scattered around your computer wherever your source files happen to be located.

(ii) Project Bundle – This encodes the MPG-2 files into your DVD Studio Pro project file. The result will be a massive project file which contains all the encoded files plus your project. This is a risky approach for the simple reason that if your project is corrupted for any reason you lose not only your project but your encoded files as well. Encoding your files into the Project Bundle could be useful if you need to move a project as a single unit from machine to machine. Otherwise this approach should be avoided.

(iii) Specified/Fallback folder – This means you choose a folder where the encoded files are to be stored. While this may sound ideal it presents its own difficulties as you will need to create a separate folder for each set of assets; meaning video files, stills, and audio.

The simplest choice is the first option: **Same Folder as the Asset**.

Leave the path set to navigate from the User through to the Desktop.

Encoding

The other preference which needs to be set is Encoding. Before we move onto the details of how to set up this preference we need to take a step back and understand what MPG-2 encoding is all about.

MPG-2 is a way of compressing video so that the video information will fit into a relatively small amount of space and at the same time maintain a high level of quality. If works by throwing away data which isn't essential to retain between different frames. All video, or film, is made up of a series of individual frames – the amount of data which needs to be written to disk varies according to the difference in the detail between each of the different frames. For example, a wide shot of a person running may include grass at the bottom of frame, the person in the middle and sky at the top of frame. From frame to frame the main change is in the person running. The sky and the grass may change very little. Therefore the Apple MPG-2 Encoder intelligently sees what changes and what doesn't and accordingly processes the information in such a way to minimize the amount of information which must be included in the overall data which is written to disk.

Now that we've got that out the way let me introduce one of the most fantastic features of DVD Studio Pro 2. You do not need to process any of your assets to MPG-2 until the point where you have structured and built all the elements to be included in your disk. In other words, you do not need to encode any of your files until the entire structure of your DVD has been put together inside of your computer. Only at this point do you need to instruct DVD Studio Pro to encode the files to MPG-2 and then to burn the disk.

What this means is you can happily work on building your project, using your assets in the form of QuickTime files (which is what Final Cut Pro and Express use) and only encode the files to MPG-2 at the end when you want to make a shiny silver disk to play in a set-top player.

Previous versions of DVD Studio Pro, and other DVD authoring applications, required the author to convert the video to MPG-2 before even beginning the authoring process. This limited creativity, limited experimentation, and forced one to be extremely organized before the DVD authoring process was even started.

While the ability to work with QuickTime files is there if you choose, you can also work in the traditional way and encode all of your files to MPG-2 before you begin working. This would be done using Compressor or the QuickTime MPG-2 Encoder. Compressor is a separate application bundled with both DVD Studio Pro and Final Cut Pro, while the QuickTime MPG-2 Encoder can be accessed from within Final Cut Pro or QuickTime Pro.

Alternatively there is a third option. You can instruct DVD Studio Pro to encode your files to MPG-2 in the background while you work on authoring your disk.

You need to choose which option will suit you best.

Now that the possible options have been explained let us look at the Encoding preference. Don't worry if everything seems a bit obscure at the moment. After all, we are talking conceptually at this stage. The practical side to making DVDs is yet to come.

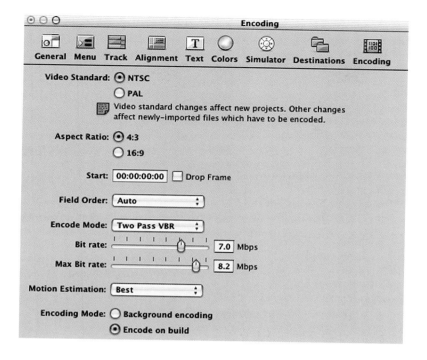

Let us start at the bottom of the Encoding preference window.

You have two options regarding Encoding. You can choose to **Encode on Build** or you can choose **Background Encoding**.

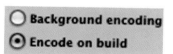

Encode on Build – This option means your assets will be converted to MPG-2 once you have completed authoring the disk. The encoding process will begin when you instruct DVD Studio Pro to burn the disk.

Background Encoding – As soon as the assets are brought into DVD Studio Pro the encoding process will then commence. The advantage is you will not need to wait for the encoding process at the end when you burn the disk. The disadvantage is Background Encoding will draw on the system resources of your Mac and potentially slow down your workflow. The degree to which this will interfere depends on which Mac you have, for example, a G4 or G5, whether it is a single or dual processor machine, and how much RAM you have installed.

The easy option is to set the preference to Encode on Build and once you have finished authoring the disk the computer will then do all the hard work for you.

If you wish, set the preference to Background Encoding and see if your Mac runs smoothly. If all is well this is a perfectly fine choice. If you find your Mac is hesitating, you frequently encounter a spinning color wheel, and everything moves in a sluggish, painful fashion, than you will know Background Encoding is not for you.

The other crucial settings to pay attention to within this preference is the video standard. This needs to be set to PAL or NTSC. You may have done this when you initially opened DVD Studio Pro for the first time. It is wise to confirm this setting. Take note of the warning: **Video standard changes affect new projects**. To play it safe set the standard and then create a new project.

The aspect ratio needs to be set: 4:3 for Standard television aspect ratio, while 16:9 is for Widescreen.

Leave the Field Order set to Auto. If you encounter problems with flicker or jerky images then you will need to investigate whether the field order needs to be set to top or bottom.

The Encode Mode must also be set.

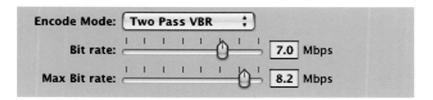

One Pass will encode the video at a constant rate. This will produce lower quality than the other options.

It is desirable to choose one of the variable bit rate (VBR) options. This means the encoding will vary depending on how much movement is taking place in the video image.

One Pass VBR will encode quicker while Two Pass VBR will take longer but produce better quality.

Choose Two Pass VBR unless you are short of time.

You need to set the Bit Rate. This is important.

In essence Bit Rate directly affects the quality of the MPG-2 video.

DVDs store 4.7 GB of data (in fact 4.37 usable gigabytes due to fact that formatting absorbs a certain amount of space). Therefore, if the MPG-2 files eat up more than this amount of space you will need a strategy to get around this problem.

The way to fit all your video material onto the disk is by adjusting the quality of the MPG-2 video. The way of adjusting this is through varying the bit rate at which the video is encoded. Bit rate is simply a unit which measures the setting which is applied to the video during the encoding process.

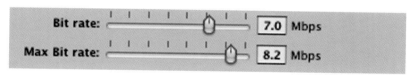

You will notice that there are two sliders. One for Bit Rate and the other for Maximum Bit Rate.

The top slider is for the average Bit Rate setting while the bottom slider relates to the maximum. All encoding which takes place, when using the VBR settings, fluctuates between these parameters. This is why the term VBR is used. When using a fixed Bit Rate, where everything is encoded at a single setting, then the Maximum Bit Rate slider will become grayed out. Only when using the VBR settings you will have the option to set both the average and the maximum.

If you are completely confused at this point, and wondering if this DVD authoring process is beyond your capabilities, relax! It is important to understand the concepts but in reality all you need to do is make a few simple choices.

To ensure the best quality set the Encode Mode to Two Pass VBR. Leave the motion Estimation setting at Best.

Now for the really important part – what to do with the sliders.

1 Keep your Max Bit Rate to 8.2.

2 60 minutes of video or less, set the Bit Rate slider to 7.0.

3 60–90 minutes of video, set the Bit Rate to 5.0.

4 90–120 minutes set the Bit Rate to 3.5.

5 150 minutes of video, set the Bit Rate to 2.0.

As would be expected, the lower the Bit Rate, the less quality you can expect.

It all comes to down to a trade-off of quality versus the amount of material you wish to squeeze onto the DVD.

Once you have set these preferences you are nearly ready to move onto the process of building your first DVD.

Simulator

You can choose to the format of the Simulator to match the television aspect ratio of your material.

Simply choose 4:3 Letterbox for standard televisions or 16:9 for widescreen.

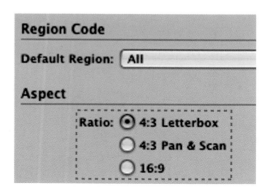

If you find the simulator to play in the wrong aspect ratio this can be easily corrected in the preferences.

CHAPTER 3
PREPARATION

Exploring the Interface

There are three different ways of setting up the interface with DVD Studio Pro:
Basic, Extended, and Advanced.

By pressing the F1, F2, and F3 keys you can cycle through these setups.

F1   Basic
F2   Extended
F3   Advanced

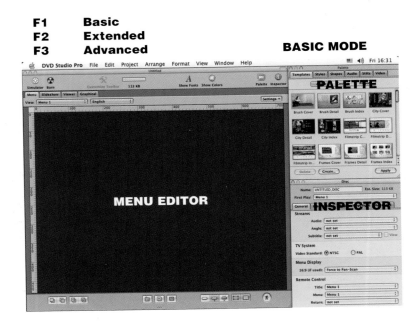

BASIC MODE

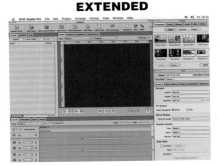

EXTENDED

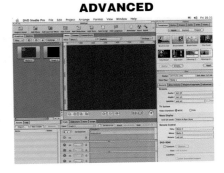

ADVANCED

The interface in Basic Mode is quite simple. There are three windows – the Menu Editor, the Palette, and the Inspector. However, this simple interface is deceptive. Underlying the three windows are a range of controls which give you the power to customize the DVD to your own specific requirements. Furthermore, one can easily jump in and out of Extended and Advanced mode or access any of these windows independently.

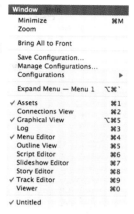

Let me reinforce this point. Just because you are working inside of Basic Mode does not mean you are limited to the capabilities of this mode. At any point you can access the individual windows found in the other modes or just as easily change to Extended or Advanced mode by simply cycling through the F1, F2, and F3 Function keys.

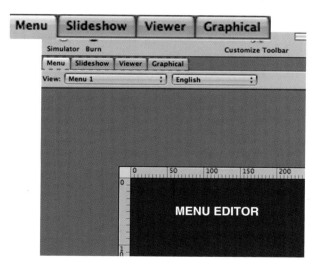

The Menu Editor is where you build your DVD. The Palette is where you access the components used to build the disk. Notice the four tabs at the top of the Menu Editor: Menu, Slideshow Viewer, and Graphical. By accessing these tabs will see visually how your menus will appear; the layout and structure of collections of still images; and in the Viewer tab you can preview any of the tracks as they are played. The Graphical View shows the relationship of each of the elements which make up the DVD.

The Palette is used for accessing any of the pre-built Templates, Buttons, Text, Drop Zones, and Shapes – under each of these heading you will find pre-built components supplied by Apple.

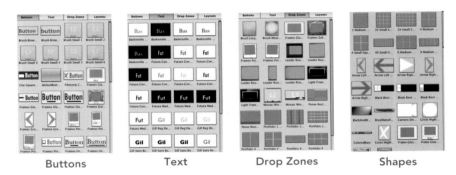

| Buttons | Text | Drop Zones | Shapes |

The Palette also serves another very important function: it is a place where you import and access the video, audio, and still files which you import into DVD Studio Pro. Notice the six tabs along the top of the Palette.

The first three – Templates, Styles, and Shapes are home to the supplied Apple components while the last three – Audio, Stills, and Video – refer to the material you bring into DVD Studio Pro.

Don't be frustrated if you cannot absorb all this in one go. It will make sense when we get onto the process of making DVDs.

Important Details About the Interface

I'm going to jump ahead here, deliberately, to introduce you to areas of the interface which you will start using soon.

First, look to the bottom right of the Menu Editor. There's an image of a man side-on profile, as if he is walking. Press this button and the result will be to start/stop the Menu. This means that any moving video (and accompanying audio) will then play. Video can be integrated into the Drop Zones, Buttons, or Menu Background.

If you have created a Still menu and have no video running as part of the menu, then there will be no result if the "man walking" is pressed.

If you are working with a Motion menu then you will see the Menu play according to how you have set it up. You may very well spot mistakes at this point, such as footage which does not start at the appropriate place or something which "just doesn't look right".

Top right there is a drop down menu titled: **Settings**. Here you will find a Title Safe Generator and Action Safe Generator as well as several other options. Leave everything at the defaults to begin with but be aware of these options for later.

Top left is **View** menu. This is a drop down menu which lets you jump to any Menu you have created.

Top middle, next to the Tool bar, is the **Disk Meter**. If you go over 4.37 GB on DVD-5 then the disk is too full. If you have a dual layer device then this presents a different story.

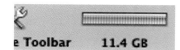

Simulator – let's watch and test your DVD before you have burnt a disk.

Effectively, the Simulator provides you with a virtual remote control.

Burn – to fire up the laser beam and cut a track of information so you can play the disk in a set-top DVD layer.

One final tip: any video or audio can be played directly in the Palette by highlighting the icon and pressing the **Play** button located bottom right, a convenient way to quickly check your assets.

PLAY   **STOP**

CHAPTER 4
ASSETS

Sorting Out Your Assets

To make a DVD you must get your assets in order. For those familiar with Final Cut Pro and Final Cut Express think of the assets as being like the files you store in the Browser. In essence, assets are the video, audio, and graphic components used in the making of the DVD.

So before you can begin the authoring process you need to get your assets exported from Final Cut Pro, or Final Cut Express, so that you can then import them into DVD Studio Pro.

Creating Reference Movies in Final Cut

As already mentioned, DVD Studio Pro will happily work with QuickTime files. It will also happily work with QuickTime Reference files which have been exported from Final Cut Pro or Final Cut Express.

Reference movies are small files which link to media already stored on hard disk. Rather than creating a separate file entirely, the reference movie simply contains information which points to the file which already exists. This provides an efficient and "space-saving" way of creating a file which can be imported into DVD Studio Pro without consuming a great deal of hard-drive space. As the name implies – Reference movies **refer** to files which already exist.

To create reference movies is a simple procedure.

1   Open up Final Cut Pro or Final Cut Express and select the sequence or clip you wish to Export in the Browser.

If you are exporting a Sequence clear the "in" and "out" points to export the entire Sequence or, mark "in" and "out" points to define the section of the Sequence you wish to Export.

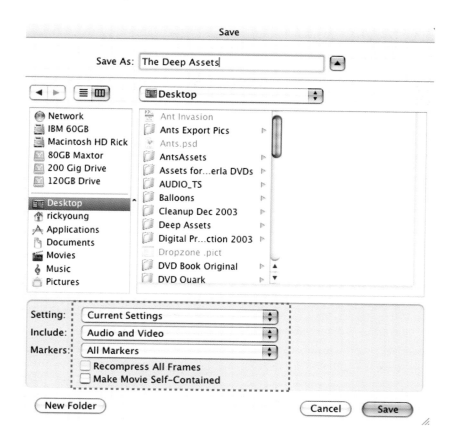

Export ▶   **QuickTime Movie...**

2   Select the File menu top left of screen and scroll to Export as QuickTime movie.

Using Compressor..
Using QuickTime C(

3   Name the file and select a location where you wish to store it. The desktop is a convenient location. You can always move it from the desktop to a location of choice once it has been exported.

For Soundtrack
For LiveType

Audio to AIFF(s)...
Audio to OMF...
Batch List...

Save

Save As: The Deep Assets

◀ ▶   ≡ ▥   🖥 Desktop ⬍

- 🌐 Network
- 🖥 IBM 60GB
- 🖥 Macintosh HD Rick
- 🖥 80GB Maxtor
- 🖥 200 Gig Drive
- 🖥 120GB Drive
- 🖥 Desktop
- 🏠 rickyoung
- 🅰 Applications
- 📄 Documents
- 🎬 Movies
- 🎵 Music
- 🖼 Pictures

- 📄 Ant Invasion
- 📁 Ants Export Pics ▷
- Ants.psd
- 📁 AntsAssets ▷
- 📁 Assets for...erla DVDs ▷
- 📁 AUDIO_TS ▷
- 📁 Balloons ▷
- 📁 Cleanup Dec 2003 ▷
- 📁 Deep Assets ▷
- 📁 Digital Pr...ction 2003 ▷
- Dropzone .pict
- 📁 DVD Book Original ▷
- 📁 DVD Quark ▷

Setting: Current Settings ⬍
Include: Audio and Video ⬍
Markers: All Markers ⬍
   ☐ Recompress All Frames
   ☐ Make Movie Self-Contained

(New Folder)   (Cancel) (Save)

4 Make sure **Current Settings** is selected; include **Audio and Video**, and if you are working with markers (to be covered later) include **DVD Studio Pro Markers**. You could choose to export video and/or audio independently by selecting **Include Video Only** or **Include Audio Only**.

5 Leave the boxes **Recompress All Frames** and **Make Movie Self-Contained** unchecked.

6 Press **Save**. Final Cut will then process this information and save the reference file to the location you have specified.

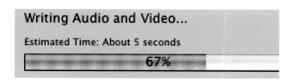

You may choose to export several reference files. If so repeat the above procedure as many times as is needed.

You could choose to create a self-contained movie. This means an entire duplicate of your film will be encoded. This takes up much more hard-drive space than a reference movie will and also takes considerably longer to create. The advantage of working with self-contained movies is that they are complete unto themselves. If you delete the original file, which a reference movie refers to, your DVD will not work. With self-contained there is less potential for trouble.

Organizing Assets

Once you have exported the assets you will work with as reference movies from Final Cut Pro you should group the assets together inside of a folder. You may have already done this during the Export stage; however, now it is the time to make sure you know where your files are. Group the assets inside of a folder and this folder can be stored anywhere on your computer so long as you know where it is located and how to access it.

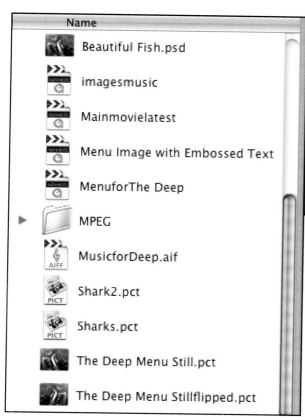

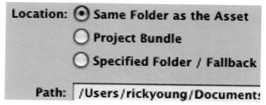

The Deep Assets

It is advisable to group your assets together inside of a folder. This folder will then be imported into DVD Studio Pro. You could set up individual folders for audio, a folder for video clips, and a folder for graphics.

You need to be organized with your assets, particularly if you have the Destination preference set to encode files to the Same Folder as the Asset. Remember, when using this method, DVD Studio Pro will create a folder titled MPG and it is here the encoded MPG-2 files will be stored. It is convenient to have these files located in a place where you can easily get to them – rather than have to search throughout your computer to determine the location of the assets to then find MPG folders alongside each of these. A single location is easier to deal with. This is basic media management.

Importing Assets into DVD Studio Pro

Now that you have created the assets in the form of reference or self-contained movies you need to import them into DVD Studio Pro. Each set of assets, be it video, audio, or graphics, needs to be brought in as a separate folder. When working in Basic Mode the Palette is used as the location to store your assets. To bring assets into the Palette a folder must be imported. It is not possible to bring individual files, one at a time, into the Palette, although individual files can be dragged directly into the Menu Editor from elsewhere in your computer.

1   Select the Video tab at the far right of the Palette.

2   Click on the + (plus) symbol located to the left of the Palette window. A window will open which enables you to navigate to the folders on your computer.

3   Navigate to the folder you wish to import.

4   Highlight the folder of choice and press Add. This will bring the folder into the Palette where it will now appear in the list at the top of the window.

5   Click the folder and its contents will be revealed visually as icons within the Palette.

Repeat the procedure for any other folders you wish to import. Multiple folders can be imported under each tab: Video, Stills, and Audio.

To the right a series of stills have been Imported as a folder under the Stills tab. When Exporting Stills as opposed to video, from Final Cut I use Export Using QuickTime Conversion found under the File menu.

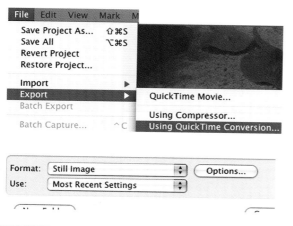

The Format needs to be set to Still Image. Under options choose Pict, Photoshop, PNG or JPG. DVD Studio Pro will work happily with any of these formats.

It is important to be aware that the files which are now accessible in the Palette provide links to the original files on hard drive. Therefore if you were to remove a folder from the Palette – achieved by highlighting a folder and pressing the – (minus) key – this will not affect the original files stored on hard drive. Nothing will be lost unless the original files are removed from hard drive. The display within the Palette simply refers to files which are located elsewhere.

Now that your assets are available you can begin the process of authoring your disk.

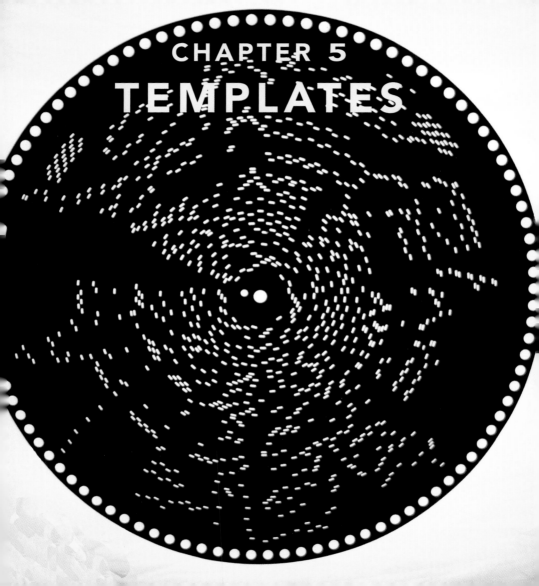

CHAPTER 5
TEMPLATES

If you want to get professional looking results, and don't want to learn all the in's and out's of creating DVDs manually, then the Templates are for you. Use the Templates and you will be able to build in all the professional components of any DVD – meaning a Motion or Still menu linking to a Main Movie, Slideshow, and Scene Index.

Many monitors display the Templates in two by two or four by four view. This gives the wrong impression of how the Templates relate to each other.

Arrange them in three by three view and the intended relationship of the Menu Templates becomes clear.

You are presented with a three-way menu structure. Most of the Templates give you a Main Movie, Additional Material, and Scene Index options.

What this means is you can feed into the Template the material you have to work with and build your DVD using a structure that is already in place.

The Templates can also be customized. Let us first run through how to use as they are before moving onto more complicated areas.

Another tip when working with Templates. If you press the third button at the top of the Palette the view will suddenly fill the screen.

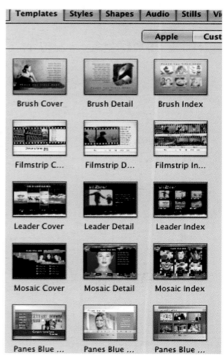

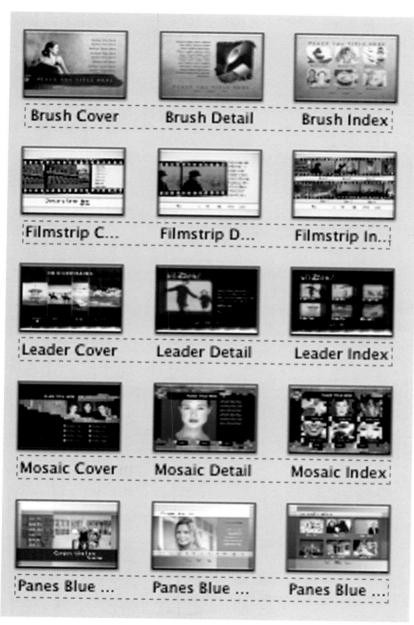

Brush Cover	Brush Detail	Brush Index
Filmstrip C...	Filmstrip D...	Filmstrip In...
Leader Cover	Leader Detail	Leader Index
Mosaic Cover	Mosaic Detail	Mosaic Index
Panes Blue ...	Panes Blue ...	Panes Blue ...

Most of the Templates provide Cover, Detail and Index Menus

You can toggle back and forth between one set-up and another.

So you can quickly get an entire overview of all the available Templates regardless of how big or small your monitor might be.

Once again click the third button at the top of the Palette to click back to the previous view. It is really as simple as that.

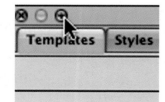

CHAPTER 6
ACTION

Making Your First DVD

Okay, we're going to do it. Now we make a DVD.

Let's run through the process before we start.

There are three fundamental steps:

1. Import the content you need into DVD Studio Pro.

2. Choose a Template.

3. Create a Track which will play the video when selected.

Now this is going to be a very basic DVD. All it will do is present the viewer with a single menu of which they have a single choice which is to play the Track.

It may come as a surprise but the simply "get it onto DVD so that people can play it" is a well-accepted way of producing disks. Many times I have been requested from clients to provide them with a single disk of a program or edited piece. They specifically don't want choices. All they want is to get their video onto a DVD to play a single section of video. They don't want or need Slideshows, Chapters, a Scene Index, or Subtitles. And they certainly don't want to pay for these. One client said to me "I just want it like VHS but on DVD". What he meant was the simplicity of VHS, not the quality!

In this situation there are two options. The easiest way is to get a standalone DVD Recorder and simply dub the program from DV to DVD. Much like hitting record on a cassette deck.

The fact is DVD Studio Pro will give you an excellent result in the three simple steps outlined above.

Put your crash helmut on. We're going into production mode.

1 In the Palette double click the Template labeled **Frames Cover**. Alternatively highlight the icon and press Apply at the bottom of the Palette.

Frames Cover

The blank Template will now open in front of you in the area of the interface known as the Menu Editor. Notice the Palette has been extended to fill the right of frame. Simply close the Inspector or extend the Palette to cover it up. For those new to DVD Studio Pro working without the Inspector, initially, can simplify the process.

2 Hold the shift key and click on all of the buttons except for Button One.

3 Press Delete so that only Button One remains.

4 Click on the single remaining button to highlight it.

5 Overtype the words "Play Movie".

6 Make sure the text is highlighted. You can now change the size of the letters and the font, if you wish. Click the Show Fonts icon located in the area termed the Toolbar. The Toolbar is located above the Menu Editor.

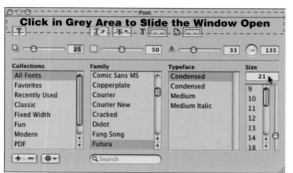

A window will open showing you the controls you have to work with.

Make sure you open the font controls to reveal the full extent of the window.

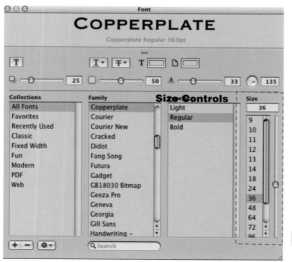

As you change the fonts the visual display at the top of the window will show you the characteristics of each of the fonts.

Size can be adjusted using the controls positioned to the right.

7 Select and resize as you wish.

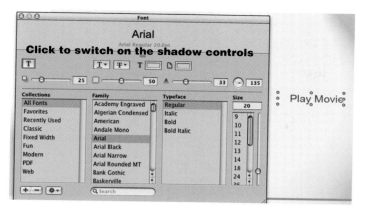

As you click-through each of the fonts, or change the size, the font display in the Menu Editor will update to show the result.

8 Click the icon titled Show Colors, located next to the Show Fonts icon which was used earlier.

A Display will appear showing the standard Macintosh color controls.

9 Choose the color of your choice. As you click-through the options the result will be displayed in the Menu Editor.

10 Once you have set the size and color you may wish to reposition the text. Switch on Button Outlines at the base of the Menu Editor. This helps.

Button Outlines

If you highlight the text and control-click this will reveal a contextual menu which lets you quickly access the text and color controls. You can also Cut, Copy, Paste, and check spelling.

Font

Size

So now you will have set the Font, the Size, and the Color.

11 Do the same for the Title Bar. Select and overtype the text and if you wish change the size, font, or color.

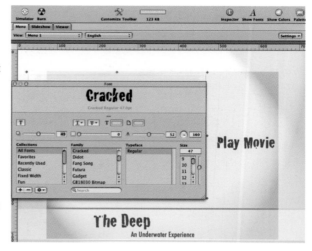

As it is the text setup with each of the Templates is well set out by default; so if you prefer you can simply overtype the text and leave the size, font, and color at the Template settings. You choose.

The next step is to add the elements to the DVD which will give it a more professional appearance. With the setup, so far, we have two areas which need to be addressed. The first is the large open space to the left of the

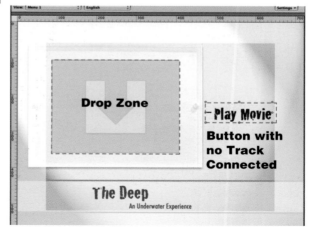

words "Play Movie". This is a Drop Zone. Here we will position a video image. The other problem is even though there is a button in place titled "Play Movie" there is currently no track connected to it. So we need to Connect a Track to this Button.

Let us first deal with the image needed for the Drop Zone.

To the right is the Palette showing the Stills which were imported earlier.

The procedure is very simple.

1 Pick up one of the images from the Palette, either Video or Still, and drag it into the Drop Zone. Do not release your mouse.

2 What is called the Drop Palette will appear. Select Set Asset. Release your Mouse button and observe the result.

Drag Image from Palette to the Menu Editor: choose Set Asset

You are now very close to having a finished DVD.

The next stage is to Connect a Track to the Button.

1 Select the Video tab at the top right of the Palette.

2 Pick up the Asset which is to be the "Main Movie" of the disk.

3 Drag the image from the Palette onto the "Play Movie" button. Don't release your Mouse button yet; wait for the Drop Palette to appear.

4 Select the third option – Create Track – Connect to Track. This will link the Button to that particular Track. Release your Mouse button.

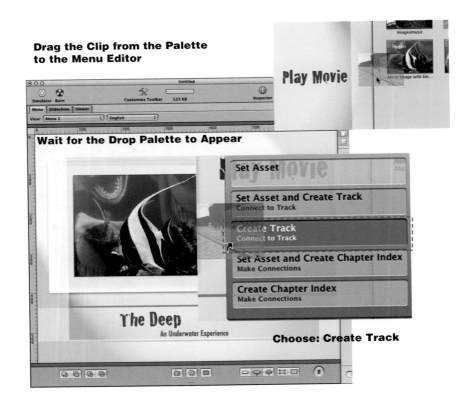

Drag the Clip from the Palette to the Menu Editor

Play Movie

Wait for the Drop Palette to Appear

Set Asset

Set Asset and Create Track
Connect to Track

Create Track
Connect to Track

Set Asset and Create Chapter Index
Make Connections

Create Chapter Index
Make Connections

The Deep
An Underwater Experience

Choose: Create Track

Have a look at the Disk Meter, located above the Menu Editor. As long as you are under 4.37 GB then you are fine.

Now, basically the disk is built. But before we burn it, and waste time and money if it's not right, we will go to a device called the Simulator. The Simulator is like having a virtual DVD player built into DVD Studio Pro so you can check out how well your disk works.

1   Press the Simulator button located top left.

If all is well the Simulator window will open a window with a black screen. After a short pause you will see the DVD menu you have been working with.

2   Press the Play Movie button on the menu which you created earlier.

Unless something is drastically wrong, the track will now play.

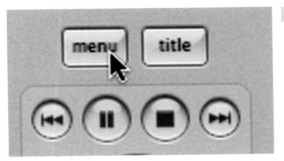

3 Press the Menu button to take you back to the main menu and, in this case, the only menu on the disk.

You could watch the track all the way through using the Simulator if you want to be extra careful, although this isn't really necessary.

4 Close the Simulator by pressing top right of the Simulator window.

Burning the Disk

Press Burn and then you wait. You wait while the machine encodes the disk. The wait while that red laser cuts data to be later decoded through the circuitry of DVD player. Depending on which machine you have, G4 or G5, single or dual processor, and how long your movie is, this could take hours, literally.

So go away and do something else. Or do something else on your computer. And when the job is done the DVD drive will open up and outcomes a DVD ready to be played in either a computer or set-top player.

CHAPTER 7
SUCCESS

You've done it. You created a DVD in using DVD Studio Pro. Now it's time to do some more disks.

Put yourself through the same process another 5–10 times.

Exactly the same.

1 Export Clips or Sequences as reference or self-contained Movies – using Export as QuickTime Movie – from Final Cut Pro or Final Cut Express.

2 Export Still images from Final Cut using QuickTime Conversion.

3 Organize the Assets inside of a folder on the Desktop or choose a location on your computer.

4 Import the Assets into DVD Studio Pro.

5 Select a Menu by double clicking the icon of your choice.

6 Highlight and delete the Tracks that are not required.

7 Using the Type Functions in DVD Studio Pro, retype and format the existing text to meet your requirements.

8 Drag any Still or Motion assets into Drop Zones.

9 Connect Tracks to Buttons by dragging Assets from the Palette to the Buttons in the Menu Editor.

10 Simulate the DVD and check if it works.

11 Burn!

The following pages are examples of simple menus created using nothing other than the Templates supplied with DVD Studio Pro.

Travel to the world's most spectacular game parks .
Get ready to enter the Kingdom of the Animals.

Adventure Bound

Examples of simple Menus produced using the Templates

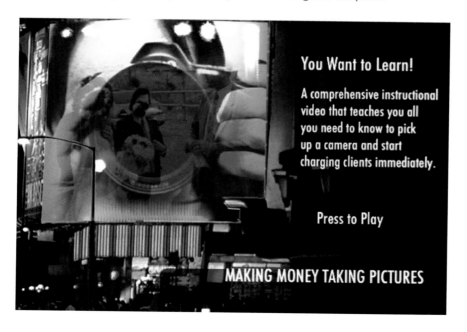

You Want to Learn!

A comprehensive instructional video that teaches you all you need to know to pick up a camera and start charging clients immediately.

Press to Play

MAKING MONEY TAKING PICTURES

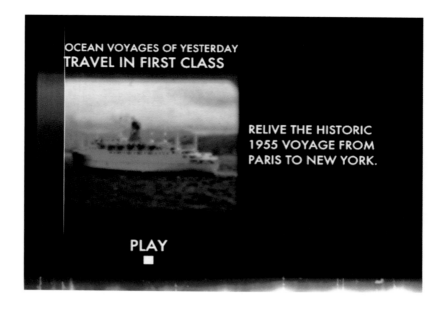

Examples of simple Menus produced using the Templates

Examples of simple Menus produced using the Templates

Creating Chapter Markers in Final Cut Pro

One of the facilities offered under the DVD specification is the ability to integrate Chapter Points within a disk. This enables the viewer to press a Button and jump to a pre-defined point. Chapter Markers are essential to have in place if you wish to build a DVD with a Scene Index.

Final Cut Pro is the application you need to open.

Open Final Cut. Make sure you have a Sequence with what will be the Main Movie of your DVD open on the Timeline.

1   Position the yellow Scrubber Bar where you wish to mark the Chapter Point.

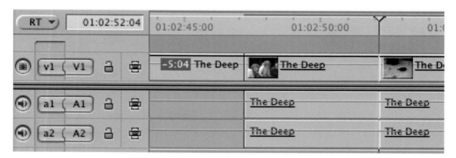

2   Press the letter "M" two times in succession. A window will open.

3   Enter a name for the Chapter Point.

4 Press Add Chapter Marker.

Add Chapter Marker

5 Press OK.

You then need to repeat the process, adding as many Chapter Markers to the Timeline as you wish.

Once you have added all the Chapter Points, the Sequence is then exported, as a Reference file, using the Export QuickTime Movie command.

This process was already explained in the section titled Creating Reference Movies from Final Cut (see page 28). If you prefer, create a Self-contained Movie instead of a Reference Movie.

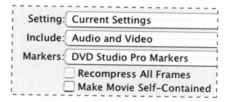

Before exporting, check that you have selected Current Settings, include Audio and Video, All Markers and leave both boxes unchecked for Recompress all Frames and Make Movie Self-Contained.

Group this file with the other Assets you plan to work with, inside of a folder which you will recall, can be stored on the Desktop or wherever you choose on your computer. You are now ready to move onto some of the more powerful features of DVD Studio Pro; the ability to work with Chapter Markers, build Scene Indexes, Slideshows and to work with multiple Tracks and Stories. But before we do all that we'll return to familiar territory and do some more work using the pre-built Templates.

Notice the green markers in the Final Cut Timeline and Canvas. These are the Chapter Markers.

Pause.

I want to talk conceptually before proceeding onto the next phase of the operation.

When using DVD Studio for creating a Main Movie and also a Scene Index, you need to be careful about how this is achieved.

One method, which may appear straightforward and easy to less experienced authors, is to create two Buttons, and to each of these connect a Track, using the Chapter Markers to define the start points of the individual scenes.

If you create your DVD using this method then you will effectively double the amount of content stored on the disk. I repeat: you increase the content by two-fold, the reason being that two tracks have been created. The Main Movie will consume the space required, and the Scene Index, which is the Main Movie broken into segments, will do the same.

Main Movie 1 Hour

Scene Index 1 Hour

Now this might not be a problem if you are producing a 5–10-minute Showreel. You could afford to encode the video at a high Bit rate and still fit all the information onto the disk.

But if you are working with a 60-minute documentary, for example, and you create a Main Movie and a separate Scene Index, you will then need to store 120 minutes which equals 2 hours of encoded video files. This means that the video then needs to be encoded at a significantly lower Bit rate to fit all of the data onto the disk.

60 minutes of video or less, set Bit rate to 7.0

90–120 minutes of video, set Bit rate to 3.5

There is a way to deal with this issue. It involves creating the Scene Index first and then targeting the Main Movie Button to the Track from which the Scene Index has been constructed.

Here's the procedure …

Creating a Menu with a Scene Index

1   Choose a Menu from the Palette by double clicking.

2   Delete the Buttons you do not need.

3   Overtype the text on the Buttons, change the color, size, and font. Nothing is connected to these Buttons, yet.

4   Add words to the Title Bar.

5   Add a Motion or Still image to the Drop Zone in the center of the Menu.

6   Drag the Main Movie, which contains the Chapter Markers, from the Palette onto the Button you will use to connect to the Chapter Index menus. Do not release your Mouse button. Wait for the Drop Palette to appear.

Main+chapters

7 Select the
fifth option:
Create
Chapter Index.
Make
Connections.

Create Chapter Index
Make Connections

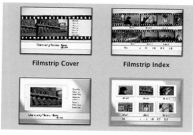

Filmstrip Cover   Filmstrip Index

8 A window will open and prompt you
to select a Template. Choose the
Scene Index Template for the Menu
you are working with.

9 Double click the Template or press
OK.

You have now created the Scene Index for the menu.
You can confirm the number of menus that have been
created by pressing the View drop-down display
located top-left of the Menu Editor. At least two or
more menus should appear in a list. What DVD Studio
Pro has done is create the required amount of
menus to house the Chapters, which make up your

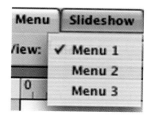

Main Movie. If you were to feed a Track containing 100 markers into this facility, obviously a great many more menus would be created.

DVD Studio Pro has done a huge amount of difficult work for you. Here's a summary of what's been done – see if you can follow it all.

When the Movie was dragged to the Create Chapter Index Function, a New Track was created and all of the Chapter Markers were imported into that Track.

Furthermore, a number of Buttons equal to the number of Chapters in the Track have been created and these Buttons have been mapped to the required number of Menus needed. Beyond this, each Button has been targeted to a Chapter Point, each Button has been renamed according to the name of each of the Chapters and a start point at the beginning of each Chapter has been set to the start point of each Asset.

And each of the Menus has controls to point you backwards, forwards, and the final Menu takes you back to the Main menu.

I don't actually expect you to follow all of this, but perhaps it will give you some appreciation of the power of this technology and what professional DVD Authors have had to do manually, prior to DVD Studio Pro being available.

Targeting a Button to a Specific Track

Now for the trick which makes the whole process work without creating two identical Tracks, thus doubling the size of your DVD.

1   Control-click the Button which will play the Main Movie.   **Play Movie**
A Menu will extend which allows you to navigate
through the structure of the DVD.

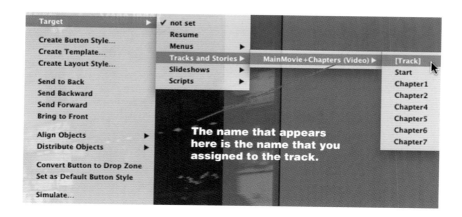

The name that appears here is the name that you assigned to the track.

2   Navigate the path that is illustrated above: Target, Tracks, and Stories; the
name of the track (Video); [Track].

You are manually targeting the Button to connect to the track which has been
used to create the Scene Index.

Once you have done this, check the Disk Meter to confirm
that you haven't exceeded the 4.39 GB limit.

2.4 GB

Before you burn you need to check that everything works.
For this you use the Simulator.

Simulator

To burn – just hit the Burn button located on the Toolbar above the
Menu Editor and follow the instructions.

Burn

Simulating

You need to get into the habit of thoroughly testing your DVD using the
Simulator, prior to burning and during the authoring process.

This is the simplest, most straightforward way to test if your DVD will work in a set-top player.

Chapter 1

Use the Simulator to move from chapter to chapter

Chapter 2

Use the virtual remote control to skip between Chapter Points. These are the same Markers that were originally entered into the Timeline in Final Cut Pro.

Chapter 3

In the case of this DVD, the Chapter Points have been used in two ways: to enable the creation of the Scene Index; and, also, to let you skip between points during the Main Movie.

Chapter 4

Both creating a movie with Chapter Points, and, Creating a Scene Index are not difficult tasks in DVD Studio Pro.

CHAPTER 8
MAGIC

DVD with a Slideshow and Scene Index

Time for the next creation. This time we are going to produce a wedding DVD. There are three sets of Templates specifically tailor made for weddings which are provided with DVD Studio Pro.

For any wedding videographer this is a perfect way to produce a professional looking disk, quickly and easily.

I've chosen to work with the middle option.

First, let us examine these Menus in detail to work out exactly what we are going to do with them.

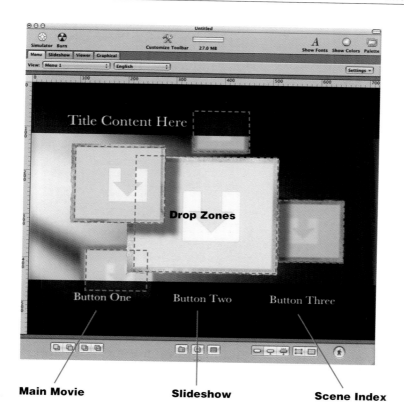

Main Movie　　　**Slideshow**　　　**Scene Index**

The first Menu is perfect for what we need. It provides the facility for three Buttons, a Title, and five Drop Zones.

Button One will play the Main Movie which will be made up of Chapters.

Button Two will connect to a Slideshow of the married couple.

Button Three will connect to a Scene Index which will be spread out over several Menus.

Each of the Menus have Drop Zones where still or motion images can be positioned.

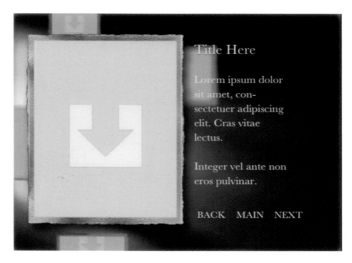

The second Menu, above, will be used in combination with a Slideshow. Exactly how it is used will be determined by how many Stills are to be included. Each Slideshow can contain a maximum of 99 still images. As always, there are work-a-rounds.

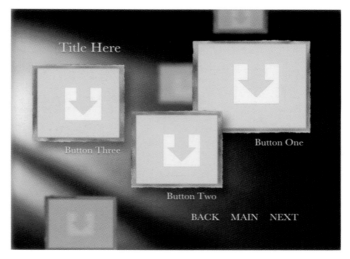

The third Menu, above, will be used to build the Scene Index. Using the tools within DVD Studio Pro each of the chapters will be put into place for you. Thus, once again, DVD Studio Pro does all the hard work.

This is what we are working to achieve. Menu One above and Menu Two below. Notice the Buttons: **Marriage, Stills, Chapters**. Nice and easy to understand. There is little likelihood of confusing the viewer.

You are now seeing Menus Three, Four, and Five. Each of these is built by DVD Studio Pro when the Chapter Index is created. The start of each Chapter is positioned onto a Drop Zone by the application.

The final Menu of the Scene Index

It should be clear that to build this DVD a series of steps will need to be followed. Here's what we are in for this time:

1 Create the Main Movie with chapters in Final Cut; create stills for the Slideshow. Import all of these Assets into DVD Studio Pro.

2 Choose the Templates from the Palette which will be used.

3 Connect the Main Movie, Slideshow, and Chapter Index to the three Buttons on the first Menu.

4 Name the Buttons.

5 Fill in the Drop Zones with motion or still images.

6 Test and Simulate the disk.

7 Burn.

CHAPTER 9
BACK TO BASICS

From the Templates in the Palette you need to first choose
and apply the Main menu for the DVD.

**Double Click
the Template
of Choice or
Press Apply**

1 Double click the Template image you
wish to select. You can also press Apply at the
bottom of the Palette.

2 Wait while the menu
is applied.

Applying Template...

3 Rename the Buttons by highlighting and overtyping.

Button One	Button Two	Button Three

The Marriage	Stills	Chapters

4 Highlight and overtype the Title Bar.

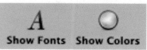

The font and color can be changed using
the controls at the top of the Menu Editor.

Make sure you have a Track with Chapters already created and exported
from Final Cut. This track must be accessible in the Palette of
DVD Studio Pro.

Now, before we concern ourselves about connecting the Main Movie to the
Button 1, titled **The Marriage**, we need to first create the Chapter Index and
then target the first button to the track from which the Chapter Index was
created. Otherwise, as already described, the video content will be doubled.
In the case of a 2-hour wedding video this would present a big problem.

Adding a Scene Index

The method which will now be demonstrated is to create the Scene Index from a track with chapter points which were added in Final Cut Pro. By creating the Scene Index **FIRST** the DVD can be authored so that the button for the Main Movie connects to the same track from which the Scene Index was created. Thus, the DVD machine will access this exact same track when playing either sections from the Scene Index or the entire Main Movie. This is logical! Understand the concept and you are well on your way.

1   Drag the Video Asset from the Palette and into the Menu Editor. Let it hover over the active part of the Button to which you wish to apply the Scene Index. Don't release your mouse.

2   Once the Drop Palette appears, choose Create Chapter Index: Make Connections.

3   A window will open. Press the third button at the top to reveal all the Template choices.

The window can be expanded to reveal all the Templates

4   Highlight your choice. You can either double click any of the menus or press OK. DVD Studio Pro will then create the Scene Index. Wait while the process is completed.

Wedding Classical In...

5   Click the tab top left of the Menu Editor to review the list of Menus. You will be able to tell straight away whether DVD Studio Pro has created the Menus or not.

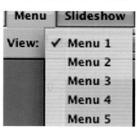

You can now flick between the Menus to see how they appear or you can go to the Simulator to run the DVD to test how the Scene Index will play in a set-top DVD player.

Adding Stills or Video to Drop Zones

Look through the Scene Index Menus and it will be clear that there are areas on each of the Menus which is still unfinished.

There are three Drop Zones on each Menu. Here either video or still images can be placed.

1 In the Palette drag video or still assets to the Drop Zone. Wait for the Drop Palette to appear.

2 Select: Set Asset.

3 Repeat for the remaining Drop Zones.

One final stage before the Scene Index is complete. The Title Bars are unfinished. Just a minor detail to fix by simply overtyping, yet if left untouched will definitely lower the professionalism of the disk you have produced.

Manually Targeting the Main Movie Button

This was already covered earlier under the heading **Targeting a Button to a Specific Track**. The same process needs to be repeated now.

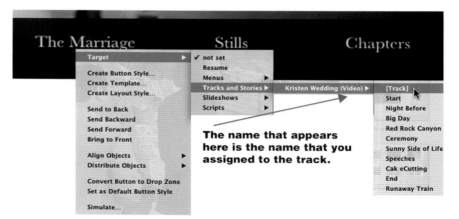

1   Control-click the first button titled **The Marriage**.

2   Navigate as is illustrated: Target; Tracks and Stories; the name of the track (Video); [Track].

3   Simulate. You can now test that when you click the button titled **The Marriage** – that it takes you to the Main Movie.

Be aware that the Chapter Points used to create the Scene Index are also embedded within the track which plays as the Main Movie. By using the controls on the Simulator you can skip between Chapters within the Track.

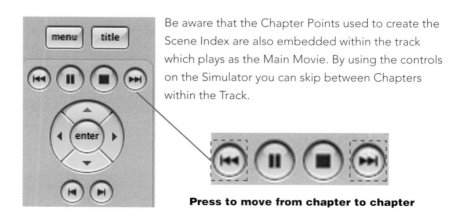

Press to move from chapter to chapter

Adding a Submenu

The term Submenu simply means "another" menu which is located further down the hierarchy of the list of Menus.

The second menu will be used as a home for the Slideshows which still have to be created.

Creating a Submenu can be achieved in a few simple steps:

1 Drag the Menu of choice from the Palette to the second button which I have titled **Stills**. Do not release your mouse button. Wait for the Drop Palette to appear.

2 Choose: Create Submenu and Apply Template.

3 Release your Mouse button.

4 Double-click the second button and the menu you selected will appear at full size in the Menu Editor.

5 Highlight and overtype any of the text for your own requirements.

You are basically taking hold of a framework that is provided and customizing it for your own purpose.

6   Fill in the Drop Zone which makes up the left half of screen. The Drop Zone is represented by the downward facing arrow. This area can be filled with still or motion video.

7   Drag a video or Still Asset from the Palette and land it right in the middle of the Drop Zone. Do not release your mouse. Wait for the Drop Palette to appear.

8   Choose Set Asset.

9   Drag Still or Video Assets into each of the three smaller Drop Zones and again select Set Asset from the Drop Palette.

10   If you are working with video assets in the Drop Zones press the **Start/Stop Motion** button at the bottom of the Menu Editor to run the video at speed.

What has been achieved is the creation of a Submenu which will accommodate one or more Slideshows. There is a purpose for having created the menu in this way. If you are confused read on – more details will become clear in the forthcoming pages.

Slideshows

So far we have spent our time working with Tracks of Video and Audio. It's now time to start working with Stills.

Back in the old days the Slide Projector was the accepted way of getting images onto a screen. In movie theatres, classrooms, and people's homes, this was the most common way to show still images to an audience.

In DVD Studio Pro Slideshows are made up of images that will play sequentially. The duration of each slide can be programmed to a specific length, or you can choose to play all slides at the same length. The Slideshow can also be set to **manual advance**, which means the viewer must forward through the stills one at a time using the Remote Control for the DVD Player. Transitions between slides can also be programmed individually or can be applied to the entire Slideshow.

Drop Audio into this area

Audio can also accompany the Slideshow. Drop an Audio Asset into the "well" which is provided. This audio track, which can be easily accessed from your iTunes library, will then accompany the still images. You can choose to force the stills to fit the duration of the audio, or, alternatively, let the audio run to the

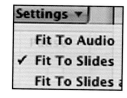

length of the stills (and loop if you wish). The audio will come to an abrupt halt if the Slideshow finishes prior to the audio finishing, so beware! Test and Simulate. This is the only way to protect yourself against such disasters before you commit the project to disk.

Don't think for a minute that Slideshows are difficult: they are not. It is as easy as importing the stills into DVD Studio Pro, selecting, dragging, and then choosing Create Slideshow from the Drop Palette.

Preparing Slideshow Assets

Before you go into DVD Studio Pro to do any work on the Slideshow, you need to be able to access the stills which will be used. DVD Studio Pro is particularly flexible and well-integrated with both Final Cut and iPhoto. You can access stills directly from your iPhoto library, and it is even possible to export stills directly from Final Cut into a folder which is also accessed by DVD Studio Pro, while both programs are open. You can then work between the two applications.

To access stills from iPhoto there are two methods.

1   Open iPhoto.

2   Highlight the stills you want for your Slideshow (now is the time to make sure they are all rotated correctly!).

3   Create and name an empty folder on the desktop or elsewhere on your computer.

4   Drag the stills from iPhoto into the empty folder.

5 Import the folder into the Palette so you can add it to the Palette in DVD Studio Pro.

The other method cuts out all the work outlined above:

1 From within the Palette in DVD Studio Pro access the stills directly through the iPhoto library.

2 Drag these stills to the Menu Editor and position on one of the Buttons. Choose **Create Slideshow: Connect to Slideshow**.

You might wonder why one would choose the first option when considering the simplicity of the second? It can be advantageous to keep all the Assets for a project together. Using the first method lets you easily group the stills into a folder where they can be stored in the same place as the other Assets you are working with.

In other situations you will need to create stills within Final Cut and then export these, so that they can be imported into DVD Studio Pro.

Exporting Stills from Final Cut into DVD Studio Pro

This is the method I use:

1   Make sure you have both DVD Studio Pro and Final Cut Open.

2   Create a folder on the Desktop or wherever you choose. Name the folder.

3   Go to the Palette in DVD Studio Pro and add this folder, using the + symbol, so that you will be able to access the folder's contents. Don't worry that there isn't anything in the folder at this stage: there will be soon.

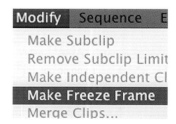

4   Open up Final Cut and place the video into the Timeline from which you will create the stills.

5   Park the Scrubber Bar on the image you wish to Export.

6   Choose **Make Freeze Frame** from the Modify menu. The frozen frame will now appear in the viewer.

7 Drag the Freeze from the Viewer into the Browser of Final Cut and name it. To keep track of the order of stills, number them sequentially starting at 01.

8 Choose the File menu at the top of screen. Scroll to Export Using QuickTime Conversion.

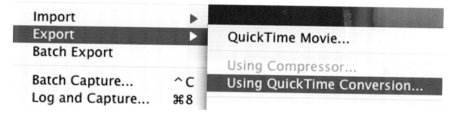

9 Check the name and navigate to the folder which you earlier directed DVD Studio Pro towards as the place to access the stills for the Slideshow.

10 Set the Format to **Still Image**.

11 Select **Photoshop, Pict, PNG, or JPG**. All of these will work.

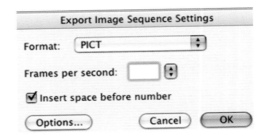

12 Press OK.

13 Press Save.

14 Repeat the process for as many stills as you need to create.

If, at any time, you select DVD Studio Pro, you can check the still assets immediately after they have been exported from Final Cut. You can thus work between the two programs, Exporting from Final Cut and into DVD Studio Pro directly, using the Asset folder on the desktop, or wherever you stored it, as the point through which all traffic must pass.

You can also **Batch Export** a series of stills. This is by far the most efficient ways of getting your stills out of Final Cut and into DVD Studio Pro.

1 Create the still in Final Cut so they are all in the Browser inside of a Bin and ready to be exported.

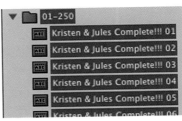

2 Highlight the stills you wish to export.

3 Select the File menu at the top left of screen and scroll to Batch Export.

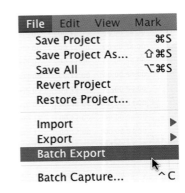

4 Release your Mouse button. The stills you had highlighted will now appear in a window titled Export Queue.

5   Click **Settings**. A window will open giving you several options. It is here that you will direct the exported files to hard disk. You also need to select the still image format for the exported files.

6   Set the **Destination**. This will direct the files to a location of your choosing.

MacPaint
Photoshop
PICT
PNG
QuickTime Image
SGI
TGA

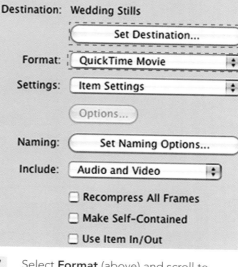

(Multiple Batches Selected)

Destination: **Wedding Stills**

Set Destination...

Format: QuickTime Movie

Settings: Item Settings

Options...

Naming: Set Naming Options...

Include: Audio and Video

☐ Recompress All Frames
☐ Make Self-Contained
☐ Use Item In/Out

7   Select **Format** (above) and scroll to **Still Image**.

8   Choose Options and set the format to either Photoshop, Pict, PNG or JPG.

9   Click Export and the list of stills will be exported, each as individual files to the folder and location which you have specified.

10   Go directly to DVD Studio Pro. If you have had both Final Cut and DVD Studio Pro open at the same time, and the folder containing the stills has been added to DVD Studio Pro, then immediately you can begin the work of creating the Slideshow.

Creating a Slideshow

1   Highlight the Assets in the Palette under the Stills Menu tab and drag these to the Button titled Slideshow. Make sure you direct your cursor to the active part of the button. The Drop Palette will now appear.

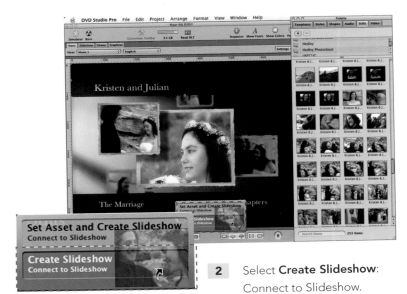

2   Select **Create Slideshow**: Connect to Slideshow.

DVD Studio Pro will now process the information and build the Slideshow.

3   Click the Slideshow Tab to reveal the list of icons, each representing a still in the list.

Slideshow Tab

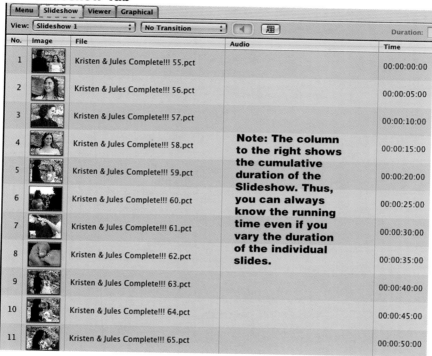

No.	Image	File	Audio	Time
1		Kristen & Jules Complete!!! 55.pct		00:00:00:00
2		Kristen & Jules Complete!!! 56.pct		00:00:05:00
3		Kristen & Jules Complete!!! 57.pct		00:00:10:00
4		Kristen & Jules Complete!!! 58.pct	**Note: The column to the right shows the cumulative duration of the Slideshow. Thus, you can always know the running time even if you vary the duration of the individual slides.**	00:00:15:00
5		Kristen & Jules Complete!!! 59.pct		00:00:20:00
6		Kristen & Jules Complete!!! 60.pct		00:00:25:00
7		Kristen & Jules Complete!!! 61.pct		00:00:30:00
8		Kristen & Jules Complete!!! 62.pct		00:00:35:00
9		Kristen & Jules Complete!!! 63.pct		00:00:40:00
10		Kristen & Jules Complete!!! 64.pct		00:00:45:00
11		Kristen & Jules Complete!!! 65.pct		00:00:50:00

4   The order of the stills can be changed. Drag the icons up and down within the list.

5   Double click on any of the icons in the list and this will lead you into Viewer. Use the Play Controls at the bottom of the Viewer to jump forwards and backwards within the Slideshow.

6   The default duration (set in preferences) can be changed for each individual slide to whatever length you wish.

7   Audio files can be dragged from the Palette into the area provided.

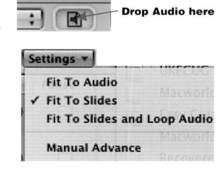

8   The audio can be set to either force the amount of slides to match the duration of the audio, or, to let the audio run to the duration of the programmed Slideshow. Be aware that if the audio runs longer than the

length of the Slideshow it will come to an abrupt stop. If the audio is shorter it will finish early. Alternatively, choose Fit to Slides and Loop Audio and the audio will loop to fill the entire duration of the Slideshow.

Now, if you return to the first Menu you will have three Buttons each pointing to separate areas.

The first Button, titled The Marriage, takes the Viewer to the Main Movie which is the edited wedding video.

The second Button, Stills, connects to the Slideshow we have just created.

The third Button, Chapters, links to the last three Menus which make up the Scene Index.

Thoroughly test the DVD. Preview all Buttons using the Simulator.

There is a slight problem. The second Menu isn't being used at all. It's as if it has bypassed altogether. When the **Stills** button is pressed, the DVD connects directly to the Slideshow. When the Slideshow was created, the button, which had been targeted to the second menu was effectively re-targeted to the Slideshow. If we refer back to the original design there were to be three menus: **Main Movie, Slideshow**, and **Scene Index**. The menu to the right is the one which is missing.

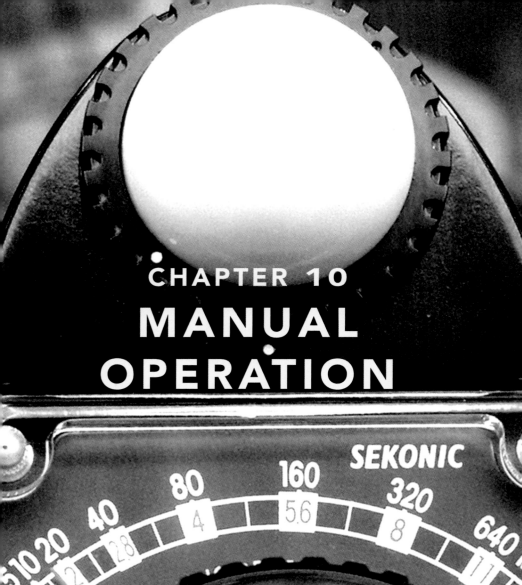

CHAPTER 10
MANUAL OPERATION

Let us assess where we are at.

So far the DVD we are creating has a Main Movie with Chapter Markers; a Slideshow; and a Scene Index.

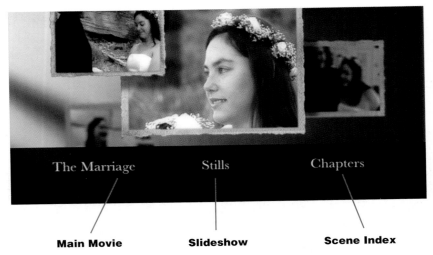

We could choose to burn the DVD in its current form and commit this to disk. The DVD will truly work, however, without the second Menu featuring a Slideshow. Instead the Button titled Stills will connect from the Main menu straight to the Slideshow.

Now one could ask the question "why even both doing another Menu? Why not leave the disk setup as is and have the second Button link to the Slideshow and leave it at that".

It depends how far you want to go with the Slideshow. One of the limitations of DVD Studio Pro is the maximum amount of stills that can be used in a Slideshow is 99. So if this number is to be exceeded then one must find a way around this limit.

There are two ways to get around this problem: first, you could convert the

95		Kristen & Jules Complete...
96		Kristen & Jules Complete...
97		Kristen & Jules Complete...
98		Kristen & Jules Complete...
99		Kristen & Jules Complete...

Slideshow to a Track and then connect several Tracks to each other (dealt with later in Advanced). Alternatively, you could build separate Slideshows which can be set up to automatically connect to the next Slideshow as an End Jump.

What's an End Jump? You ask. The End Jump is where the DVD goes next

End Jump: [**Menu 2::Slideshow 3**]

when an Asset, such as a Track or Slideshow, finishes. The End Jump can be manually targeted.

By connecting Slideshows one can literally have hundreds of stills play in succession.

Slideshow 1 will connect to Slideshow 2 and Slideshow 2 will connect to Slideshow 3.

Each of the three Slideshows will house 80 or more stills. This would not be possible in a single Slideshow.

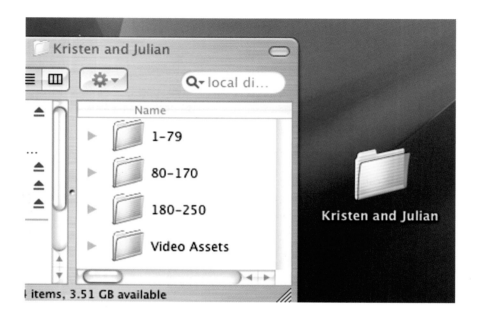

In this instance I am working with a total of 250 stills. To organize this large number of slides I have created three folders in the Assets folder for the project and then grouped 80+ stills into folders within the main Assets folder. The individual folders for still images will then be imported into the Palette of DVD Studio Pro.

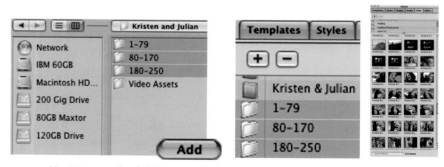

Navigate to the folders you wish to import. Hold shift and click to select multiple folders. Press Add to import.

The Inspector

So far we have ignored one of the major parts of the interface: the Inspector. This window sits close to the Palette, though the Palette can be extended to obscure the Inspector or the Inspector can be repositioned or closed.

The Inspector can be accessed by simply pressing F1 to assume the Basic interface setup. You can also click on the Inspector to make it active. Alternatively, if it has been hidden from view, choose the View menu and scroll to Show Inspector.

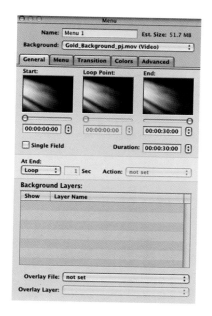

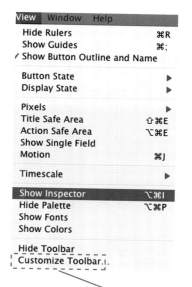

The Inspector is what I call "multi-functional" which means it does a lot of things.

The best way to understand the Inspector is to start using it. Click on different areas within the Menu Editor and, at the same time observe the Inspector. When you click on a Button, a Track, a Menu background, a Slideshow, each time the Inspector will react by giving you a different set of controls. The Inspector is a powerful part of the interface which should not be ignored.

Also notice the **Customize Toolbar** option at the bottom of the View menu. By selecting this option one can then arrange specific tools at the top of the interface.

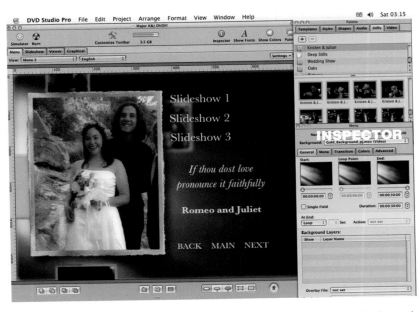

Here's just a short list of what the Inspector can do for you: connect Audio and
Video Assets to Buttons, Tracks and Slideshows; change the Highlight color of a
Button; adjust the Start Frame of an Asset; reposition text with Buttons, name
the DVD, rotate and format text, add and set the duration of transitions, choose
between Still and Motion menus, name your Menus, Tracks, Slideshows, modify
shapes and set End Jumps. In short, the Inspector does a lot of different things.

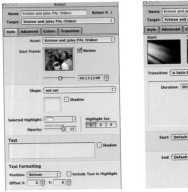
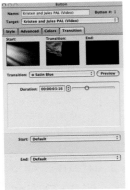

Some of the many faces of the Inspector

Customizing the Toolbar

The Toolbar is the
strip that runs along
the top of the interface above the Menu Editor.

Toolbar

1   At the top of the Menu Editor press
Customize Toolbar or control-click in
the gray area of the Toolbar. This will
reveal a Contextual menu.

2   Once you have chosen Customize Toolbar
a window will open showing all the tools
that can be placed on the Toolbar for
easy access. Drag a Tool from this window
onto the Toolbar.

3   Press done when you have added the
items you need to work with.

4   The configuration can be saved. Select the
Window menu, scroll to Save Configuration.

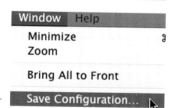

5   Name it.

6   Save it.

> **Different window configurations can be saved to suit different working environments or styles.**
>
> Name your current workspace:
>
> **Rick**

If you look in the list of Configurations under the Window
menu you will find your named setup, which can be
accessed by pressing F5 or by highlighting and clicking.
Choose the Window menu and select Manage
Configurations to delete a configuration you have created.

Rick basic	
Basic	F1
Extended	F2
Advanced	F3

Manage Configurations...

Individual items which you place on the Toolbar can be
removed by control-clicking and pressing Remove Item.

Remove Item

Fine Tuning the DVD

Now back to the Wedding Disk. We are so close to having completed this disk, but there are a few details to take care of before it is ready to Burn.

We have to create another Menu, create Buttons to connect to the Slideshows on this Menu, and then target each End Jump so that when a Slideshow finishes it will "invisibly" move onto the next Slideshow. It is now time to move beyond the Templates and to start manually targeting Tracks, Buttons and Slideshows. This is one step beyond simply dropping material onto pre-built Templates and letting DVD Studio Pro do the work for you.

First of all, let's make sure each of the Assets used in the Drop Zones on each of the Menus starts at the correct point.

Remember, Motion or Still Assets can be used for each Drop Zone. If you have used Video then you may wish to adjust the start point of the Video Asset:

1 Make sure the Inspector is open.

2 Click on a Drop Zone.

3 Look to the Inspector: if the Drop Zone contains a Still Asset there will be no facility to adjust the start or end point, however, if it is a Video Asset then you will have controls for the start points.

You can also choose for the Asset to be Motion or Still.

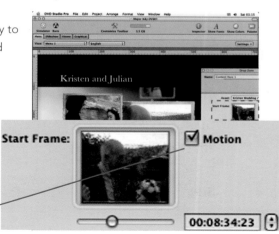

Now let's try something different:

1 Click on the Title Bar to make the controls active in the Inspector.

2 Glance towards the Inspector. Make it active if necessary.

3 You can rotate, enter, format, and adjust text using the Inspector controls.

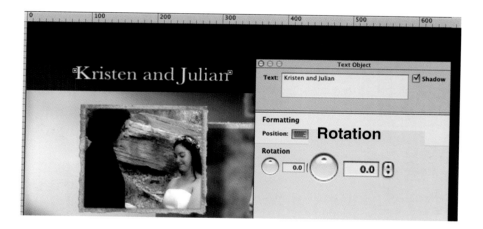

The Inspector gives you the power to customize and control the look of the DVD menu. As you change attributes in the Inspector, it will update in the Menu Editor.

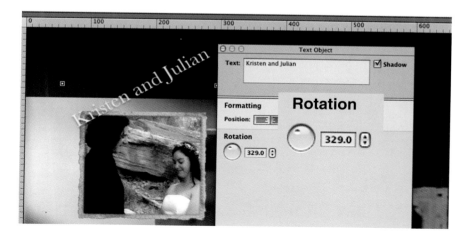

In combination with the Text controls in the Toolbar the size and shadow attributes can also be altered. These techniques are particularly useful when building menus from scratch without using the Templates.

The power of DVD Studio Pro lies in the control it gives you over the authoring process. Beyond this, the quality of the MPG-2 encoding is excellent.

Manually Targeting Assets

When working with the Templates, DVD Studio Pro does a lot of work in the background which the beginner would not be aware of what is taking place.

For example, in Basic Mode, when you drop a Track onto a Button not only is the Track then connected to that Button but also the End Jump is targeted back to the Menu where the Button resides.

It is very useful to be able to override the default action of DVD Studio Pro and to manually target Track, Buttons, and Slideshows to wherever you want them to go. It is not difficult to target the End Jump of a particular Asset.

Return to the Main menu for the Wedding DVD which features three Buttons – I'm sure you have seen enough of this one by now.

The center Button titled Slideshow needs to connect to Menu 2. At the moment it links to a Slideshow. This needs to be changed.

1 Click on the active part of the Button.

2 In the Inspector click the drop down menu next to the word Target.

3 Scroll to Menus.

4 Scroll to Menu 2.

5 Select [Menu].

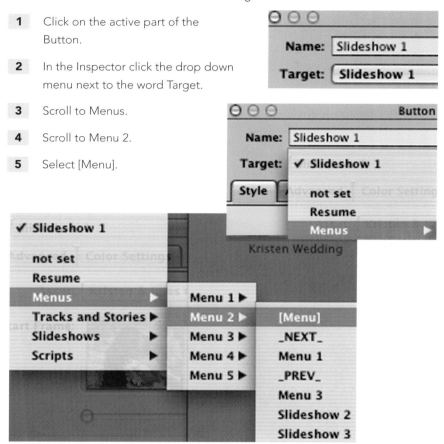

What you have just done is targeted that Button, when pressed, to link to Menu 2. The word [Menu], enclosed in square brackets, indicates that the target is set to a Menu which is titled Menu 2.

The same can also be achieved by control-clicking on the active part of the Button. A Menu will appear. Select Target and navigate to the Menu of choice. You can also manually target Tracks, Slideshows and other devices such as Stories and Scripts.

Control-click on a Button to Target it Manually

So now if you go to the Simulator you can test that the Button titled Stills actually connects to Menu 2.

Final Touches

A final review of exactly where we are and what remains to be achieved.

Menu 2 as it Stands

The Final Result

The first task we need to achieve is to add three Buttons to Menu 2 which will be used to link to each of the Slideshows.

Return to Menu 1, the Main menu. For uniformity we will copy the Button Style prior to beginning work on Menu 2. This will facilitate design consistency and also make the overall task easier when we get to the next phase of the operation.

Creating Button Styles

We have yet to explore the wonderful world of Buttons. They come in all shapes and sizes and are one of the integral tools which you have to work with.

As there are so many variations of what Buttons look like, how they "light up" when activated, whether they feature an Asset or not, it can be useful to copy a style and know that the design will be uniform from Button to Button and Menu to Menu.

1 Highlight the active area of the Button from which you wish to copy the attributes.

2 Control-click the Button and scroll to Create Button Style. A window will now open top right of the interface.

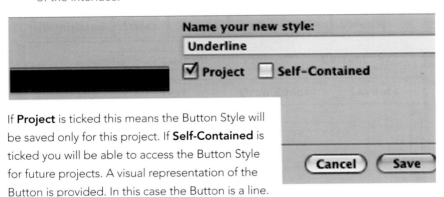

If **Project** is ticked this means the Button Style will be saved only for this project. If **Self-Contained** is ticked you will be able to access the Button Style for future projects. A visual representation of the Button is provided. In this case the Button is a line.

3 Name and Save the Button Style which can then be

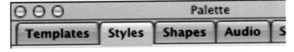

accessed from the Styles tab. You need to choose Buttons then Project or Custom depending on where and how you saved it.

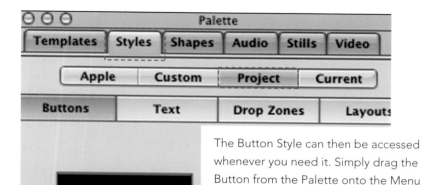

The Button Style can then be accessed whenever you need it. Simply drag the Button from the Palette onto the Menu Editor to create a new Button. Button Styles you create can also be deleted. Highlight the Button in the Palette and press Delete located bottom left of the Palette.

Adding Buttons

Adding Buttons is as simple as drag and drop. Let's just make sure we are on the right Menu before we start.

1 Return to Menu 2.

2 Highlight and delete the Title which reads Slideshow. It will not be needed.

3 Pick up a Button from under the Styles tab and drag it onto the Menu Editor and wait for the Drop Palette to appear.

4 Choose **Create Button: Set Style** from the Drop Palette. The Button and Text in the style from Menu 1 will now be on screen in front of you.

5 Repeat the process another two times to make a total of three Buttons.

6   Highlight and overtype each of the Buttons naming them Slideshows 1, 2, and 3.

7   Click **Button Outlines** and/or **Guides** at the base of the Menu Editor. This will make the Buttons visible as they will be when active and the guides provide a grid to align objects with. Working in this mode can help with moving and positioning of Text and Buttons.

You may have noticed when you initially positioned the Buttons that the active part of the Button sits immediately below the words.

Button Outlines/Guides

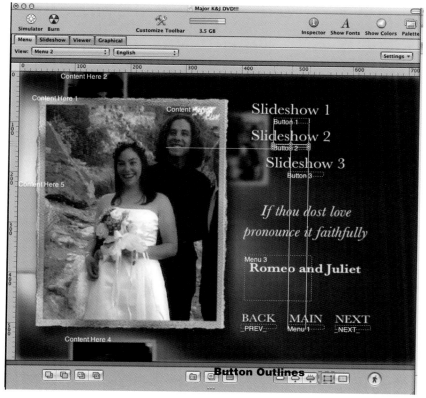

This can be easily repositioned and modified precisely using the controls in the Inspector.

1   Make sure you can see the Inspector in front of you and that the first tab titled Style is selected.

2   Click on the active part of the Button.

3   Look to the bottom of the Inspector to the Text formatting box. Text can be entered here directly. Click the Drop Down menu.

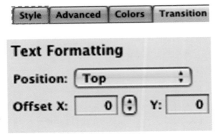

As you alter the parameters in the Inspector the result will appear in the Menu Editor.

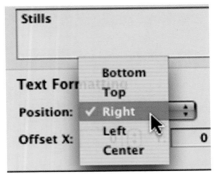

4   Use the X and Y offset controls for fine adjustments.

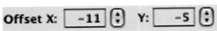

5   The result is the active part of the Button is now located to the right. If you tick the box in the Inspector: **Include Text in Highlights,** then the text will "light up" at the sametime as the active area of the Button.

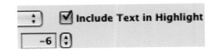

Use the horizontal and vertical arrows for precise positioning of text in the Menu Editor. Use drag and drop, by all means, but be aware the arrow keys will give precision which is difficult to achieve in any other way.

Creating Slideshows

The Menu now consists of three Buttons, each titled, however there are no Assets connected.

Audio	Stills	Video
Kristen & Julian		
1-79		
80-170		
180-250		

1   Go to the Palette and click the second to last tab titled Stills.

2   Click the appropriate folder for the first batch of Stills which you wish to use for a Slideshow.

3   Drag the Stills to one of the Slideshow buttons. Wait for the Drop Palette to appear.

4   Choose **Create Slideshow: Connect to Slideshow**.

5   Double click the Button and the Slideshow will be displayed under the Slideshow tab. Scroll to the bottom of the Slideshow to reveal the number of stills.

6   Create a total of three Slideshows each connected to separate Buttons. The fact is, you will now have an additional Slideshow which is not connected to anything, this being the original Slideshow which had been connected to the second Button. If you wanted to make use of this it could be manually targeted to one of the Buttons on the Menu we are presently working with.

Targeting Slideshows

If you're still with me the situation is as follows: everything is in place except that the three Slideshows need to link to each other. Slideshow 1 needs to End Jump to Slideshow 2, which, in turn, needs to End Jump to Slideshow 3. And Slideshow 3 will return to the main Menu.

Piece a cake.

1 Double click the active area of the first Button which is Slideshow 1. This will lead into a display of the Slideshow in Icon view.

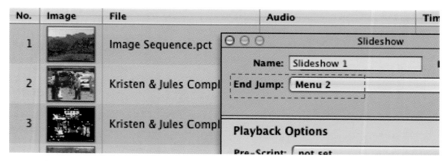

Notice the End Jump in the Inspector. This needs to be set to jump to Slideshow 2.

2 Click on the End Jump drop down display and navigate to Slideshow 2.

3 Repeat the procedure for the Button for Slideshow 2, only this time have the End Jump set to Slideshow 3.

4 For the final Slideshow the End Jump needs to be set to connect back to Menu 1.

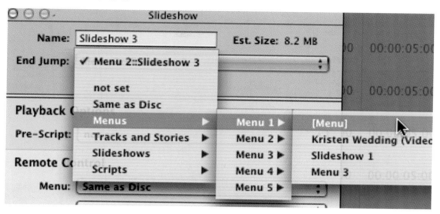

If you have difficulty with any of these procedures make sure that each time you wish to set the End Jump of a particular Slideshow you first go to the Menu tab at the top left of the main window (in the Menu Editor) then double click the active part of the Button. This will lead you into the Icon display for the Slideshow. Make sure the Inspector is active and then reset the End Jump to the desired target.

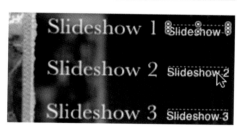

Note: If you switch on Button Outlines at the bottom of the Menu Editor this may make it easier to see exactly where the Button is positioned.

Setting Audio Assets for Menus

Now I'm not sure if anyone has noticed, but this Wedding DVD has no audio connected to any of the Menus. It would be a nice touch to have some sort of audio play each time a different Menu is selected.

I would suggest preparing the audio in Final Cut, or another audio application, so that it will run the duration you require for the length of each Menu. It is not possible to program in fades within DVD Studio Pro. The overall Menu duration can be set in the Inspector.

Audio Assets can be accessed directly from your iTunes library, under the Audio tab, or you can export audio from Final Cut as an AIFF file.

1 Simply click on the Menu background (in the Menu Editor) and set the

duration in the Inspector. If it is a Still menu you are working with you can ignore this.

2 Pick up an Audio Asset from the Palette, drag it onto the background of the Menu to which you wish to connect it, and

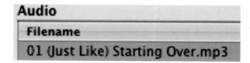

then choose the command from the Drop Palette, Set Audio.

3 Once the Audio Asset is in place press the Start/Stop Motion button to hear the result.

Click the Menu tab in the Inspector and the Audio Track is then displayed.

> **Audio**
> **Filename**
> **01 (Just Like) Starting Over.mp3**

Finally...

1 Test and Simulate to make sure everything works.

2 Once you are happy – Burn!

CHAPTER 11
BUTTONS

Let's talk about Buttons.

Remember, right at the beginning of this book, I made the statement that DVDs are made up of Menus and Tracks. To get to those Tracks you must click on a Button. It's as simple as that.

Buttons are the mechanisms through which you access the content on the DVD. In terms of functionality, that is what they do. However, in terms of design elements, Buttons offer a world of possibilities.

This is where it starts to get interesting. Bundled with DVD Studio Pro is a wide range of Buttons for you to choose from. You could say they come in all shapes and sizes.

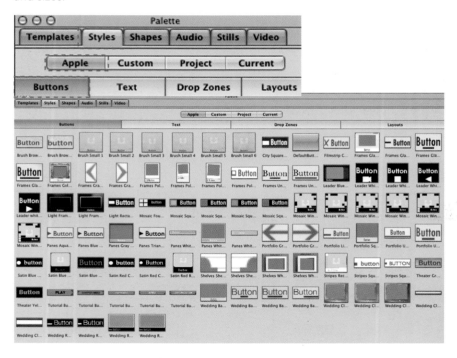

To make use of the Buttons, you must understand that there are two different types: first, Buttons to which an Asset can be connected, and second, Buttons which function on their own without an Asset. Assets can be moving Video or Still images.

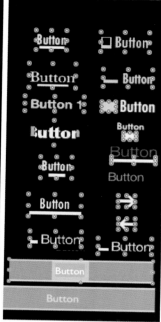

Buttons connected
to Assets

Buttons that do not
connect to Assets

Those new to DVD Studio Pro often have problems understanding what the Button is actually doing.

To test a Button and see how it works, you need to first select it from the Palette.

1 Select the Styles tab.

2 Check Apple is selected.

3 Check Buttons is selected.

4 Choose a Button and drag it from the Palette into the Menu Editor. Do not release your Mouse button. Wait for the Drop Palette to appear.

5 Choose **Create Button: Set Style**.

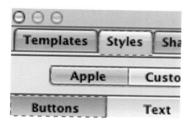

You will recall from the work we have done so far that buttons "light up" so-to-speak when they are pressed.

Each Button has three possible states: the most important being the **Selected** state. This state indicates to the user that the buttons is "selected" and ready to be pressed.

Normal – This is the state when the Button has not been pressed or selected.

Selected – When one uses a remote control, the four arrows direct the equivalent of a cursor between each of the Buttons on-screen. The Button is selected with the remote control using the four arrows.

Activated – The Button has been pressed! The Activated state is usually a short burst, prior to a track or Slideshow playing, or wherever it has been targeted.

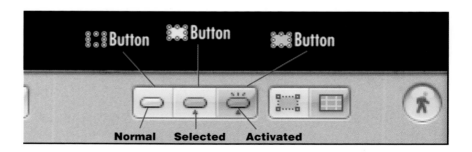

Viewing the possible states of the Button can be achieved by:

1 Highlighting the Button in the Menu Editor.

2 At the base of the Menu Editor, click through each of the three buttons indicated in the diagram above. Each state, Normal, Selected, and Activated can be previewed for any of the Buttons.

Once you have clicked the Button in the Menu Editor, look to the Inspector. Click the Style tab at the top of the Inspector.

The Inspector shows you the attributes of the Button and provides you with the controls. At the top of the Inspector is the title Button.

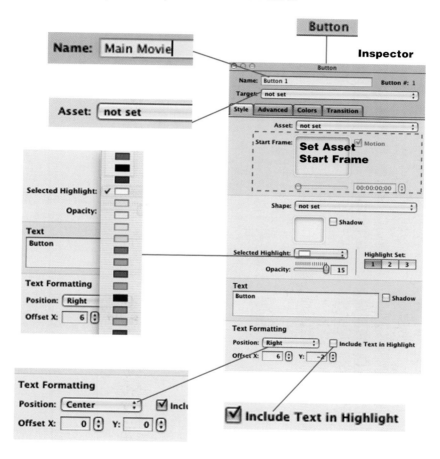

1   The Button can be named in the Inspector.

2   The Button can be manually targeted to a particular Asset.

3   If it's a Button which has an Asset connected to it, then the start frame of the Asset can be set.

4   The color of the button's Selected or Activated highlight can be modified using the controls in the Inspector.

5   Text can be positioned in relation to the active area of the button. This can be precisely controlled using x and y co-ordinates.

6   By checking the box **Include Text in Highlight** means, the text will react in the same way as the Button for the three states of activity: Normal, Selected, and Activated.

It can get quite deep technically at this point if one begins to investigate what goes on under the surface. It's sufficient to say that you can change the colors of the button in each of the Active states, plus you can also adjust the level of opacity.

Another way to preview what a Button is doing, is to jump straight into the Simulator and roll your mouse over the Button. A mouse isn't a remote control but it will give you a good idea of what to expect. This works, whether the Button is connected to an asset or not.

Of course, the Button can be renamed. Simply highlight and overtype, whatever you like.

The following pages will be devoted to showing the buttons visually and how they appear, in a practical sense. You will see examples of Buttons used in conjunction with Assets and also examples of Buttons, which do not accept Assets. Once this is understood we will move onto investigating the relationship between Buttons, Shapes and Drop Zones. Buttons are there to add to the Menu Design. It is therefore worth getting a general overview of the range and types you have to work with.

Buttons which Accept Assets

Button without Asset

With Asset Connected

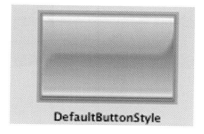

DefaultButtonStyle

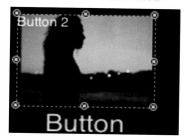

Frames Glass Small ...

Frames Gold Small F...

Frames Polaroid Me...

Button without Asset

With Asset Connected

With the release of DVD Studio Pro 3 several new buttons
have been added to the collection of Apple buttons.

Button without Asset

Frames Polaroid Me...

Frames Polaroid Me...

Leader Blue Rough R...

Panes Gray Rectangle

With Asset Connected

The assets above are converted to black and white with a blue cast. Several buttons treat the image through adjustments to color or softening of the picture. Buttons which make use shapes in this way are called Patches.

Button without Asset

With Asset Connected

Panes White Rectangle

Portfolio Square Win...

Shelves White Frame...

Shelves White Frame...

With some Buttons it is difficult to know the result without adding an Asset to see the result. Experimentation is the key.

Buttons without Asset   **With Asset Connected**

Shelves White Frame...

Shelves White Frame...

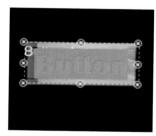

Theater Yellow Text

Wedding Band Blue ...

Prior to DVD Studio Pro being available such versatility was unheard of. Apple have built compositing capabilities into a DVD authoring package.

Button without Asset	With Asset Connected

Wedding Classical G...	

Wedding Classical G...	

Wedding Classical G...	

Wedding Rect Small ...	

Several of the Buttons frame the image and convert it to
black and white or sepia.

Button without Asset

With Asset Connected

There is nothing difficult about the concept of working with Buttons.

To add a Button to a Menu, just pick it up from the Palette, drag it to the Menu Editor, and when the Drop Palette appears, choose **Create Button: Set Style**.

If you want to delete a Button just click on it and press the Delete key on your keyboard.

Buttons can be resized in the Menu Editor. Click the Button to make it active – circles will appear at each corner and on the center of each side.

Hold the Shift key while resizing to constrain proportions.

If you do not constrain the proportions, and the Button has an Asset connected to it, then the Asset will be cropped. It will not appear unnaturally distorted as no distortion of the image takes place.

123

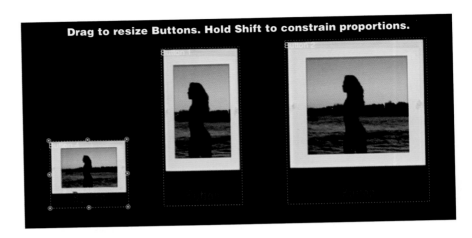

Press the Start/Stop Motion menu to see the result. You can drag and resize the Button while the images play.

To add an Asset, Still or Motion, to a Button – obviously this can only be done to a Button which works with Assets – then simply pick up the Video or Still asset from the Palette, drag it above the button's "active area" in the Menu Editor, then from the Drop Palette select: **Set Asset.**

Set Asset

To set the Asset and at the same time also create a track which the Button will connect to, choose: **Set Asset and Create Track: Connect to Track.**

Set Asset and Create Track
Connect to Track

To connect a Track to a particular Button, select **Create Track: Connect to Track.**

Create Track
Connect to Track

The options to **Create Chapter Index**'s are also presented.

Set Asset and Create Chapter
Make Connections

Create Chapter Index
Make Connections

Basically you need to decide, do you want an Asset set for the Button; or do you wish to Create a Track or Slideshow without an Asset featured as part of the button. The option is there to do either.

So far we have investigated the Buttons that have Assets connected to them. Now I'm going to present an overview of the other Buttons, made up of shapes: circles, squares, oblongs, and arrows.

Buttons which do not work with Assets

There are more Buttons that do not work with Assets than will.

All of the Buttons which, do not work with Assets can be dragged and resized and, unlike Buttons which do accept Assets, the shape of the Button will distort as you drag it. This is most useful as it allows one to create Button shapes by distorting a shape already provided. The colors for the active state can also be changed.

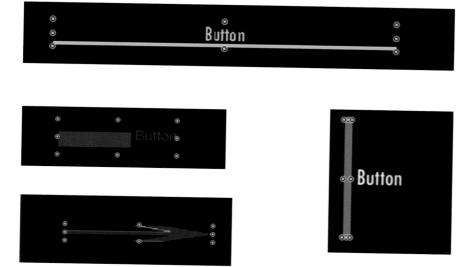

Most of the Buttons that do not work with Assets give a result that is relatively close to the image presented in the Palette. However, as always, there are a few exceptions. See the following images for a few of the Buttons that do not accept Assets and how they appear, once used.

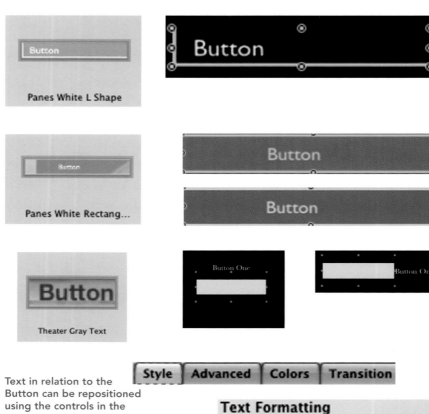

Panes White L Shape

Panes White Rectang...

Theater Gray Text

Text in relation to the Button can be repositioned using the controls in the Inspector. Make sure you have selected the Style tab at the top of the Inspector.

For the new user, it can be difficult to work through each and every Button, which is available. While the Buttons are listed alphabetically, it takes a while to get to know them all and how they can be used, particularly when you consider that Drop Zones and Shapes can also be used as Buttons.

What this means is that there are a lot more Buttons available than those which are listed under the heading Buttons.

Time to investigate Drop Zones and Shapes.

Working with Shapes and Drop Zones

You are probably feeling all "buttoned out" by now.

Let's strip it back to basics just to remind ourselves what we are dealing with.

A Button is used to connect to "somewhere else" on the DVD. That "somewhere" could be an Asset, such as a Video Track, or a Menu, or a Slideshow, for example.

Buttons come in two types:

1 Those which can have an Asset connected to the Button.

2 Buttons that function without Assets.

There are two other areas which relate to Menu Design which also relate to Buttons: these are Drop Zones and Shapes.

All **Drop Zones** can be used to run moving Video or Still images as part of the Menu Design. Drop Zones can be converted into buttons.

Within DVD Studio Pro are pre-built Shapes. These **Shapes** have characteristics associated with them. The Shapes can be used as Buttons or Drop Zones. As with the Buttons we have already investigated, some, but not all, can have Assets connected to them.

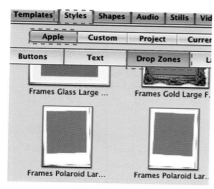

Drop Zones

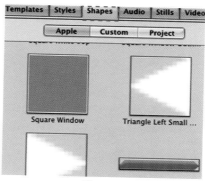

Shapes

Drop Zones are accessed from the
Styles tab in the Palette. You then
need to select Apple and
Drop Zones.

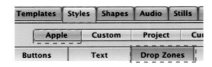

Shapes are accessed from the
Shapes tab in the Palette.

Now listen for the really important part. **Drop Zones and Shapes can be used
as Buttons**.

When a Drop Zone is dragged onto the Menu
Editor you are given only one choice: Create
Zone. However a Drop Zone can be easily
converted to a Button.

When Shapes are dropped onto
the Menu Editor you are given a
choice to create a Button or a
Drop Zone.

Shapes and Drop Zones will have
characteristics associated with them. Some
will be transparent, some will have a border,
and, if Assets can be connected, then different effects to the video image will
be applied.

The DVDs produced earlier with the Templates are all made up of no more
than a Background, Shapes, Drop Zones, Buttons, and a Title Bar.

Marked in red on the following pages are Shapes that work with Assets. Those
Shapes that are not marked, do not work with Assets. All of the Drop Zones
work with Assets.

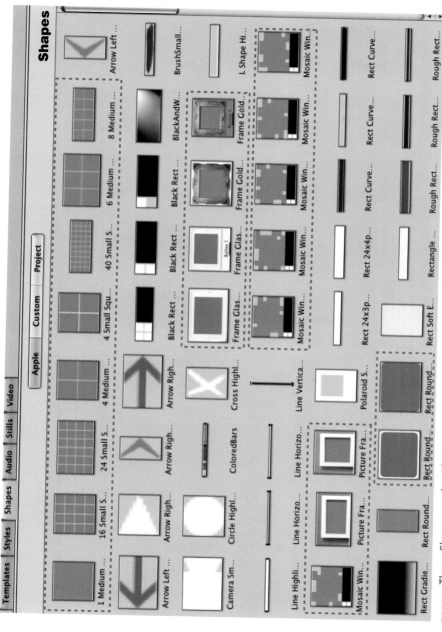

- - - - - These Shapes work with Assets.

------ These Shapes work with Assets.

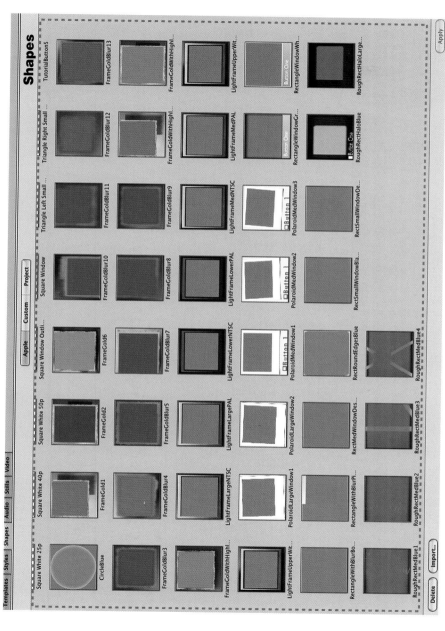

----- These Shapes work with Assets.

131

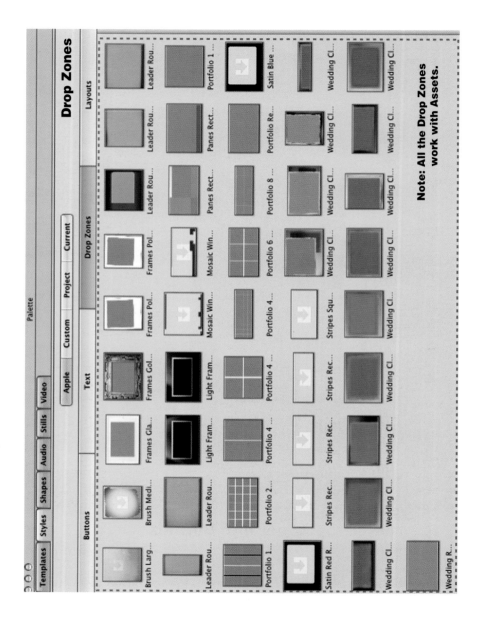

Drop Zone 1

Target

Create Drop Zone Style...
Create Template...
Create Layout Style...

Send to Back
Send Backward
Send Forward
Bring to Front

Align Objects ▶
Distribute Objects ▶

Convert Drop Zone to Button

Converting Drop Zones into Buttons

1 Control-click on a Drop Zone in the Menu Editor.

2 From the contextual menu which appears, scroll to **Convert Drop Zone to Button**. The Drop Zone then becomes a button displaying whatever asset has been previously set.

Examples of Drop Zones in action

Examples of Shapes (used as Buttons) in action

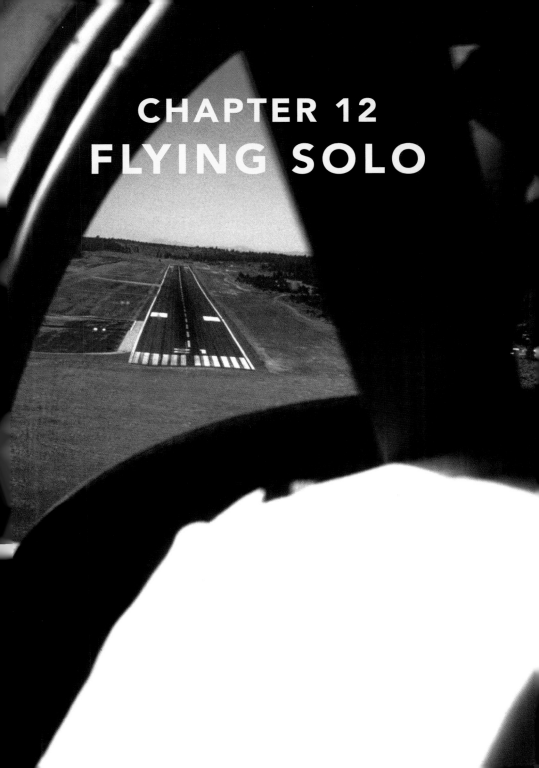

CHAPTER 12
FLYING SOLO

Working without Templates

Let's throw away the training wheels and start working without Templates. It really isn't that much harder creating DVDs from scratch than it is using the Templates as a framework to build with. The main difference is that you, the author, has to work that little bit harder to make your DVD look good. The big advantage – the DVD will be unique. When using Templates anybody can achieve a result and the disk produced will look the same except for content, assets in Drop Zones, and the wording on the Title Bar, perhaps. Without Templates – it all comes down to pure design ability.

The design of the Menu is paramount. This is what the viewer sees first when the DVD is played onto a television. Each Menu is made up of two or three components: a Background, Buttons, Drop Zones, and a Title Bar. Of all of these the Background is what stands out the most.

Setting the background is easy. Choose, first, whether you are going to create a Still or Motion background. If still then you can happily work with Pict, Photoshop, PNG, or JPG images. If motion video, my way of working is to edit the background together in Final Cut Pro, perhaps slowing down or changing the color of the images for effect. I also edit a Soundtrack at this stage. There is far superior control to match sound with picture inside of Final Cut than you will ever find in DVD Studio Pro. This edited footage, with audio, is then Exported as a Reference or Self-contained Movie, imported into DVD Studio Pro, and dropped into the Menu as a Background.

There are several steps which need to be followed to create a DVD menu manually. Presented below is an overview of the process:

1   Set the Menu's Background.

2   Add a Title Bar.

3   Position Buttons.

4   Add Assets to the Buttons (if the Buttons work with Assets).
Note: Buttons can be duplicated. Position a single button and then press
Apple+D. The duplicate Button can then be repositioned.

5   Create Tracks, Slideshows, and a Scene Index, if required, and connect
these to the Buttons.

6   Test and simulate.

7   Burn.

Creating Menus, Slideshows, and Tracks

Menus, Submenus, Slideshows, and Tracks can each be created by dragging items from the Palette to the Menu Editor.

These can also be created by pressing the icons at the base of the Menu Editor. Check the end jump in the Inspector to confirm it will take you back to where you wish to go.

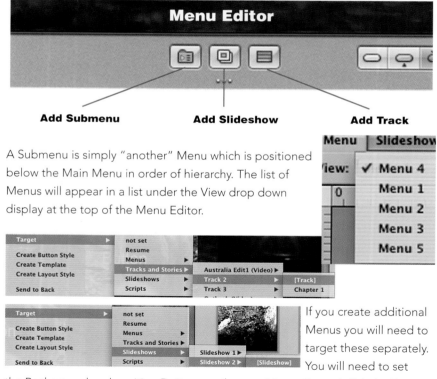

A Submenu is simply "another" Menu which is positioned below the Main Menu in order of hierarchy. The list of Menus will appear in a list under the View drop down display at the top of the Menu Editor.

If you create additional Menus you will need to target these separately. You will need to set the Background and position Buttons on the new Menu. Control click the Buttons to reveal the targeting controls or you can target Tracks, Menus or Slideshows with the Inspector.

Setting the Background Image

This has got to be one of the simplest and most rewarding actions you will perform with DVD Studio Pro.

1 Drag an Asset from the Palette to the Menu Editor. Wait for the Drop Palette to appear.

2 Choose the first option: Set Background.

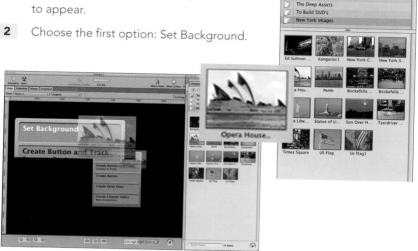

You can easily change the Background as many times as you like. Just drag and drop Video or Still Assets onto the Drop Palette and choose Set Background.

You can use different Assets for different Menu backgrounds within the same DVD. You need to decide how many Menus your DVD will need. Many DVDs work well with just a single Menu.

Adding a Title Bar

Now that the Background is set you need to add a Title Bar to identify the DVD. The easy way is to double-click anywhere within the Menu and then type the words you require. Alternatively:

1   In the Palette, at the top, Select the Styles tab. Check Apple is selected and choose Text.

2   Pick up any Text Object and drag it onto the Menu Editor and wait for the Drop Palette to appear.

3 Choose the first option:
Create Text Object.
Set Style.

4 Highlight the Text and
overtype.

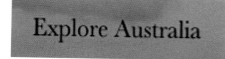

Once the words are types select the Show Fonts and Show Colors controls from the Tool Bar to adjust the font, size, and color detail.

Using Shapes as Drop Zones

To make the Text stand out I wish to create a transparent mask below the Title. By accessing the Shapes I can create a Drop Zone which will sit below the words and above the Background.

1 Make sure you have selected Shapes at the top of the Palette.

2 Scroll through the list of Shapes until you locate those titled Square Navy. These are transparent and this transparency can be used for effect.

3 Drag the Shape from the Palette to the Menu Editor. Choose **Create Drop Zone**. **Set Shape**.

Square Navy 40p

4   Position the Drop Zone above the Text Object.

5   Use the **Bring to Front** and **Send to Back** controls at the bottom left of the Menu Editor to adjust the hierarchy of layers for the Menu. Highlight the object, be it Text, Button or Drop Zone, and press the controls and observe the result.

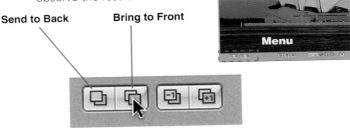

Send to Back   Bring to Front

Creating and Positioning Buttons

I need to create three Buttons for this disk. Two of these will connect to Tracks, the other to a Slideshow:

1   Go to Styles-Apple-Buttons in the Palette. Choose a Button and drag it to the Menu Editor.

2   Choose: Create Button. Set Style.

To create further Buttons you can either repeat the above process or highlight the Button and press **Apple+D** to duplicate.

Once your Buttons are created simply drag them into position within the Menu Editor. Name the Text by highlighting and overtyping or use the Inspector.

Adding Assets to Buttons

Now, remember from our in-depth discussions about Buttons, there are the kind that will accept Assets and those that will not. So, assuming the Button you are working with will accept an Asset simply drag that Asset from the Palette, Video or Still, to the Menu Editor and select **Set Asset**.

Now you have a choice here – in fact you have several choices.

You can simultaneously Set the Asset to the Button and Create a Track will then play when the Button is activated.

You can create a track, thus leaving the Asset for the Button not set or set to another asset.

Experiment. That's how you will learn.

Further down the Menu one moves into the territory of Chapter Indexing.

My strategy for creating Chapter Indexes is to only do so using the Templates. You need to select a Template from which the Index will be created. Once created you can then change the Background, the Button Style, Text – everything about it. To manually create a Scene Index from scratch would take a lot of work and technical knowledge.

One of the strong points of DVD Studio Pro is that it lets you quickly change your mind about the DVD you are making. Traditionally, all the assets were prepared

The Buttons can be resized and all the elements juggled while the Assets within the Buttons and the Background play in real-time. Press Start/Stop Motion.

well in advance, all the Menus were put together, every still accounted for … you could say the "DVD production line" was a bit more rigid than it is now.

Creating Tracks

In the last few pages we covered how to add assets to Buttons that will accept them. Once that phase of the process is sorted you need to connect Tracks to the Buttons.

It's a two-step operation:

1 Drag the Asset to use as a Track from the Palette to the Menu Editor.

2 Hover your cursor above the Drop Palette, scroll to **Create Track**. **Connect to Track** and release your mouse.

The Track will now be connected to that particular Button. If you go to the Simulator you can test that the Track plays when you press the Button. Repeat the process for any more Buttons you wish to connect Tracks to.

Creating a Slideshow

Another easy-to-perform operation:

1 Highlight the Still Assets in the Palette.

2 Drag these to the Menu Editor and hover over a Button until the Drop Palette appears.

3 Select Create Slideshow. Connect to Slideshow.

If you then double-click on the Button in the Menu Editor this will then take you into the Slideshow window where you can set the duration of stills and add audio.

Test and Simulate

At any time jump straight into the Simulator and see what's working and what's not working with your DVD. You need to test and simulate regularly throughout the authoring process. It's not like you put it all together and then Simulate at the end to make sure that it's right; rather you check the usability of the disk within the Simulator many times throughout the production of a DVD.

Simulator

And if it checks okay in the Simulator then you know what comes next.

Burn

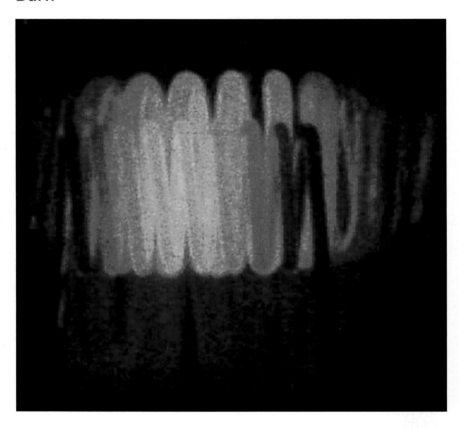

CHAPTER 13
THE GREATEST
TRICK OF ALL

The Greatest Trick of All is to make your Menus look good.

That pretty much surmises my philosophy for DVD creation. Spend the time to get the Menu right, choose your fonts carefully, play with the image to see what can be done, do all the crazy effects you ever wanted to, or just have a plain still sitting there looking at you. You decide.

Television commercials are designed to catch your attention.

So is the case with Menus.

It doesn't matter how you do it so long as you don't make the viewer want to switch off the Television.

Lead the viewer to the content and their attention will focus on the DVD itself and the authoring process will be transparent behind the cloak of the Menu.

And step outside of DVD Studio Pro. Build your Menus using Final Cut Pro and the other applications bundled with it: such as LiveType and Soundtrack. You have a whole suite of applications to author with. Why restrict yourself to just one?

Even once you have created a Menu, it can be radically changed in just a few swift moves.

The following Menu designs feature three Buttons each with Assets, a Background and a Title Bar. The second Menu has the same three Buttons, although slightly resized, and shows a different Background with the Title Bar now being integrated into the background video.

Simply changing the Menu background can produce a very effective result. You may wonder how the words Explore Australia, in the second Menu, were created?

It was all done between Final Cut Pro and LiveType. The text was created in LiveType and then exported: this file was then imported into Final Cut Pro where it was positioned over the lizard.

An effect is applied as the words appear. The entire piece was then positioned in the Final Cut Pro Timeline and edited so the end frame and the start

frame are identical – thus allowing for a seamless loop when the DVD plays the Menu.

To take the whole process one step further, a 20 second looping piece of music was created using Apple's Soundtrack application. All of Apple's software pulls together to provide a complete suite of authoring tools.

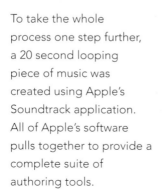
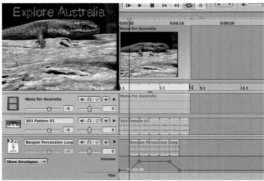

Once all the elements have been put together between Final Cut Pro, LiveType, Soundtrack and any other application you may use, then the movie is exported as a QuickTime Reference Movie from Final Cut Pro. This is then imported into DVD Studio Pro.

Export	▶	QuickTime Movie...

The authoring process goes beyond DVD Studio Pro and beyond Final Cut.

There are people out there using Photoshop, After Effects, Boris Red, Combustion, Commotion and a host of other packages and plug-ins. You can use DVD Studio Pro on a very basic level and create stunning results. Particularly if you add a little shine and glitter from a third-party plug-ins or applications.

Get the Menu looking good; choose a nice background image; provide easy access to the content. These are the *golden rules* of DVD authoring.

Making a DVD is virtually as simple as setting a background, creating buttons, and connecting tracks.

And don't forget printing and packaging. If you want your disk to look professional then buy yourself one of those printers that print directly onto DVD. You can't do it any other way. Stickers cause DVDs to be unreliable on playback, and writing with a pen just doesn't look very good. Certainly not to paying clients.

Check out the following pages for a Menu I created for DVD titled The Deep. The Angelfish was too good to be true. I ran a ripple through the image in Final Cut Pro and keyed over some text that also has a ripple effect, although at a different speed to the main image.

So simple yet, striking.

The Final Cut Pro Timeline for this Menu is made up of the elements of the composited effect and an audio Soundtrack. By creating the Visuals and Audio together, inside of a single Timeline, both can be exported a single reference file. When this is imported into DVD Studio Pro sound and video come in together. This is a simple and effective way to get picture and sound to marry up exactly as you want them to be.

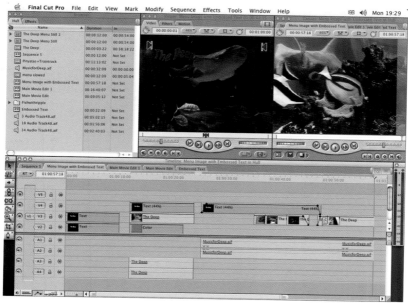

The idea behind this book is to open your eyes to what the world of DVD has to offer. This is by no means the definitive guide. In fact in many ways it only teaches the very basics of what DVD authoring is about. But it teaches the core commands that will get you up and running. And when you are ready to take the knowledge further, then you jump into the other modes, Extended and Advanced, and use DVD Studio Pro to its full potential.

CHAPTER 14
ADVANCED

Press the F3 key located towards the top left of the keyboard. This will take you into Advanced Mode.

Basic Mode   **Extended**   **Advanced**

You can shift between each of the modes by pressing the Window menu and scrolling to **Configurations**.

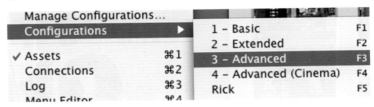

The Advanced interface is made up of six windows. Before you start getting panic stricken that this is the way over your head, sit back and realize that you are already familiar with several of the windows. To the center and right are the Menu Editor, and the Palette and Inspector. Top left is the Graphical View.

Next to the Graphical tab is the tab which will take you to the Outline window. This is an important tool for you to work with as it provides an overview of the structure of your DVD.

Outline View – Selected by clicking the tab to the right of Graphical. In Outline View you can rename Menus, Tracks, and Slideshows. You can juggle the of order Menus, Tracks, and Slideshows. You can also name the Disk. Items can be deleted from the Outline View by highlighting and pressing Delete. This is important. Once deleted the memory being taken up for that particular asset will then reclaimed.

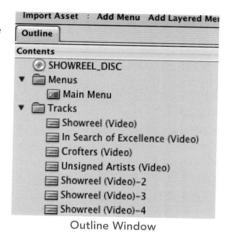

Outline Window

Assets – This provides an overview of the Assets that have been imported into your project. Assets can be dragged directly from the window into the Menu Editor or the Track Editor. Note that DVD Studio Pro recognizes these Assets as separate Video and Audio files. When a Video track is dragged to either the Menu Editor or the Track Editor, the associated audio will follow.

Track Editor – Part of the versatility and appeal of DVDs is the power of the format to read data quickly from disk.

Assets Window

As the viewer sits there pressing buttons on the remote control they want things to happen straightaway. You, the DVD author, pre-empts what the viewer will do. One of the tools for ordering and structuring material inside DVD Studio Pro is the Track Editor. In short the Track Editor lets you edit clips together; add chapter points, add multiple streams of Audio, Video, and Subtitles. These are professional level functions which you may or may not wish to get involved with.

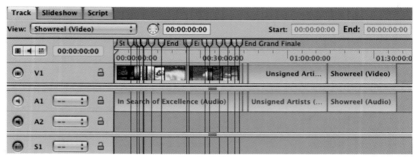

Track Editor

Advanced View

Advanced View provides you with a range of controls that are simply not there in Basic Mode. By working in this mode you get the full picture of what is going on with your DVD.

At any stage, at the press of the F1 button, you will then be in the familiar territory of Basic Mode.

The fact is, you can access all of the windows in Advanced from within the Basic Mode by simply choosing the Window menu and calling up the window of choice.

Don't forget to Simulate, don't forget to Save, and remember Apple+Z to undo or Apple Shift Z to redo.

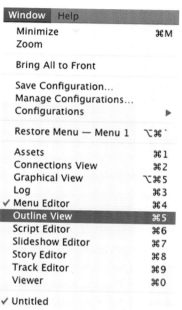

The additional windows provided in advanced
can also be accessed within Basic

Working in Advanced Mode

When it comes to working in Advanced Mode you can either continue using all the methods and techniques you are familiar with from Basic Mode, or you can jump up a level and treat the whole authoring process with a different mind-set.

For example, in Advanced you do not need to go through the laborious method of importing folders into the Palette to then drop these one by one onto the Menu Editor. Instead you can lift assets one at a time, or in groups, directly from any location on your computer, and import these directly into the Assets window. The same can be achieved by pressing the Import button.

All the Tracks, Slideshows, and Menus used in your project are listed in the Outline View. Here you can get an entire overview of all the components that make up the DVD. These can easily be ordered according to level of priority. For example, simply drag a Menu up or down within the list of Menus and the order displayed in the Outline View will be reflected in the list of Menus found under the View tab in the Menu Editor.

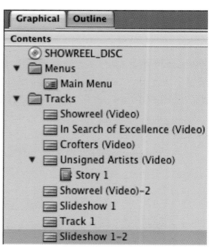

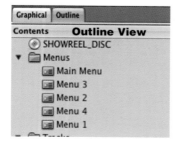

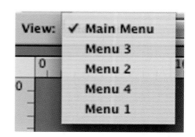

You will recall when the Encoding Preferences were set that a decision was made about the bit rate at which the video would be encoded to MPG-2. In Basic Mode it is possible to run into trouble when one has set the bit rate and then made use of assets to find that the Disk Meter has shot well past the limit of what a DVD can hold.

14.7 GB

The way to deal with this problem is to lower the bit rate at which the material is encoded. However, before you reset the bit rate you need to first step into the Outline View, one of the windows available in Advanced Mode, and highlight and delete the Asset. This will then reclaim the space on the DVD (This can also be achieved using the Graphical View, dealt with later.). Once this has been done you need to reset the bit rate. Outline View can also be accessed in Basic Mode, by choosing from the Window menu. Advanced Mode provides you with a more powerful interface to Basic so it makes sense to use this facility. Jumping in and out of windows isn't always the most elegant way to get work done.

Then there are stories. Stories give you the ability to reorder the contents of a track using chapter points to define sections within the track. This allows for different "cuts" of a film to be stored on the same DVD without actually taking up any more space. For example, the European and American release of a production could be included; offensive material could be deleted for particular screening requirements. This means the same track can then be played in a different order without adding extra content to the DVD.

Beyond this, there is copyright protection which can be set in the Inspector. Be aware copyright management will only work for professionally authored disks. An Apple Superdrive or consumer DVD burner cannot write the copyright protection information.

The big player in Advanced Mode is the Track Editor. This is easy to use and powerful. It lets you add functionality to your DVD. Using the Track Editor one can author multiple streams of Video, Audio, or Subtitles. The Track Editor also provides the ability to add, move, and delete chapter points within a track.

Master Advanced and you will have entered the realms of professional DVD authoring. And don't be shy to jump back into Basic if you feel inclined. Whatever it takes to get the job done.

Another tip – there is another mode called Extended – press F2. This gives you a nice big Timeline in the Track Editor to work with.

Basic

Extended

Advanced

Outline View

This presents an overview of your disk.

This is where you name the Menus, Tracks, and Slideshows. Then this gives you the power to properly manage your assets. The Outline window does what it says – it gives you an outline of all the components that make up your DVD.

The hierarchy of Menus can be reordered in Outline View.

Grab hold of a Menu and slide it up or down within the list of Menus and release your Mouse button.

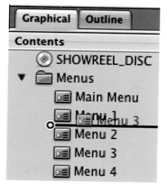

The change is reflected in the drop down View display.

Double-click on any of the assets.

For example, double-click a Track in the Outline window and it will appear in the Viewer. When you play the Track the display in the Track Editor follows the visuals. It should be clear that these windows work together, rather than independently. Each window should not be seen in isolation, rather as part of the overall interface.

To delete any of the assets displayed in Outline View highlight and press Delete.

As mentioned earlier the space taken up on the DVD by that asset is then reclaimed. If your bit rate was set too high, and therefore using up too much space on the DVD, you could then reset the bit rate to a lower setting to enable you to fit the encoded Video files onto the disk. This can be achieved through the Encoding Preference.

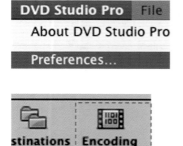 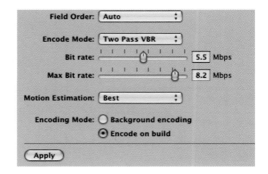

Another very quick and simple method to set the Encoding Settings is to Control-click on the Track you wish to encode in the Assets window.

Choose Encoder Settings from the menu which appears. Once the Bit rate has been reset, simply drag the asset back into Outline View. This content will then be added to the DVD.

Note: To check the overall amount of space which is used on your DVD refer to the Disk Meter located to the right of the Toolbar.

Assets Window

All your assets are listed alphabetically in an area that is very much akin to the Browser in Final Cut. You can import Assets, create folders – very much the same concept as Bins in Final Cut – and you can remove folders and assets by highlighting and pressing the Remove button.

Think of the Assets window as being a container which holds all of the elements you use to make up your DVD: Video, Audio, and Stills.

If you extend the Assets window – click between the Track Editor and Assets window, and drag with the tool that appears…

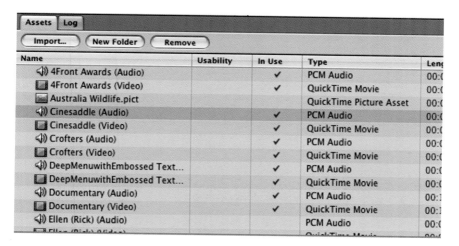

…then you will reveal other useful information such as which Assets are in use, their duration, and size.

Also notice the Usability column. When Background Encoding has been selected in preferences a usability light will appear displaying the encoded status of each Asset.

Name	Usability	In
▼ 📁 Australia Clips		
🔊 Ants (Audio)	⊖	
🎞 Ants (Video)	⊖	
🔊 Ants1 (Audio)	⊖	
🎞 Ants1 (Video)	⊖	
🔊 Australia Edit1 (Audio)	⊖	
🎞 Australia Edit1 (Video)	⊖	
🔊 Australia Edit2 (Audio)	⊖	
🎞 Australia Edit2 (Video)	⊖	
🔊 Australia Edit3 (Audio)	⊖	
🎞 Australia Edit3 (Video)	⊖	
🔊 Bridge (Audio)	⊖	

Green – Encoded.

Yellow – Yet to be Encoded.

The advantage to encoding the Assets in the background is that when you come to burn the project to disk the process will be much quicker as the encoding has already taken place. Furthermore, you will know whether the material will fit onto the disk as it has already been encoded.

Control-clicking on any of the Assets opens a Menu with several options. These are powerful functions that need to be investigated:

Import Asset – This provides a quick way to import Assets without selecting the Import button.

Create New Folder – I'm sure you can work this one out for yourself.

Encoder Settings – As mentioned earlier here one can set the Encoding Preference. This is a powerful tool. It

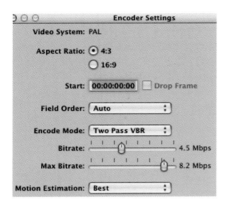

means you can set the bit rate for a particular asset, drag it into the Outline window, check the Disk Meter to see how much of the DVD has been filled up. If it is over the limit of what the DVD can accommodate, bearing in mind any other assets still to be added, then simply delete the Asset from the Outline window. You then reset the bit rate and drag the Asset from the Assets window into the Menu Editor where it can be used within the structure of your DVD.

Preview Asset – The Asset is then previewed in the Viewer in the center of the Advanced interface. The same can also be achieved by double-clicking on an Asset within the Assets window.

Re-Link – If an asset has been moved from the location where DVD Studio Pro expects it to be then use this function to re-establish the link. Similar to Reconnect Media in Final Cut Pro.

Refresh – When the original Asset is modified use the Refresh command to update in the Asset you are working with.

Reveal in Finder – Takes you to where your asset is stored within your Mac. Very useful for locating where your assets are stored.

The Track Editor

The Track Editor is where the real action happens. Keep in mind, however, when working with DVD Studio Pro that no particular area dominates over another: rather everything works together. While authoring you will continually move from the Inspector to the Menu Editor to the Track Editor and each of the other windows as you need them.

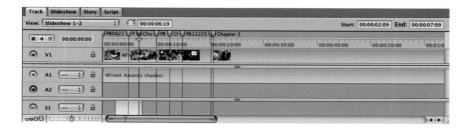

In terms of functionality the Track Editor offers a lot.

Here's a summary of what you can do:

1   Edit up to nine streams of Video, eight streams of Audio, and 32 streams of Subtitles.

2   Add, delete, and move Chapter Markers.

3   Convert Slideshows to Tracks.

4   Edit Tracks and Stills together in a single stream or edit multiple sections of Audio together in a single stream.

It is important to understand when working with independent streams that this is not the same as working with separate tracks of video or audio as one would in the Timeline in Final Cut.

If you are old enough to remember eight track tapes from the 1970s, then the concept is similar. With eight tracks it was possible to flick between individual or stereo tracks while the tape was playing. The tape was wide enough to hold eight independent tracks. Independent, but not all accessible at the same time!

So it is with the Track Editor in DVD Studio Pro. You would only ever watch one Video stream at time, or listen to one audio stream, or watch one set of Subtitles. A bit like switching channels on a TV.

Working with the Track Editor

The project that is open in Outline View shows all the components that make up the DVD of my Showreel. There are six tracks, each of which are connected to individual buttons. What I want to do is to create a Track which plays all the six individual clips in succession. The Track Editor provides a means of achieving this.

6 Tracks, each of which can be played individually, or which can be played in succession by pressing the Play All button.

Before I begin I want to warn you the method I am presenting is not the most efficient method that could be used. It will cause the doubling up of material on the DVD as was explained in depth earlier in this book. But for the purposes of this project, which contains only a small amount of Video material, this is workable method. Aside from this, you will get a good overview of the capabilities of the Track Editor and the functionality it offers.

1   Press Add Track in the Toolbar at the top of the interface.

2   A new Track will appear in Outline
         View.

3   Name the Track by overtyping.

4   Click the Track and it will become
         active in the Track Editor. At the moment it is empty as nothing
         has been added to it.

5   Drag an Asset from the Asset window into the Track Editor. Release it, and
         video and audio will appear in the Timeline of the Track Editor.

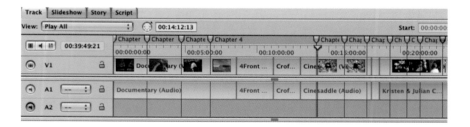

6   Drag more Assets to join with the end of the Track already in place in the
         Track Editor.

Tracks will be added to where ever you drop them. Thus if you drop a Track
between two existing Tracks the Track being positioned will perform the same
function as an Insert edit in Final Cut – that is the Tracks beyond it will be pushed
further up in the Timeline.

At any time you can preview the Track that you have in the Track Editor. Make sure the Viewer tab has been pressed at the top of the Menu Editor and then use the virtual controls at the base of the Viewer to play, stop, or move forwards or backwards a frame at a time. You can also use the Space Bar to stop/start and familiar controls at the bottom of the Track Editor, obviously modeled on the Final Cut interface, which give you the ability to expand and contract the size of the Track you are working with.

As in Final Cut, Shift Z will condense the overall spread of the Track. Holding down the shift key and pressing the horizontal arrows will allow you to skip through the track one second at a time.

7 The Track you have created will appear in the Outline window. This needs to be connected to a Button. Drag the track from the Outline window to a Button of choice in the Menu Editor. Use the Drop Palette to connect the Track to the button.

8   Double-click the Track for it to open
in the Viewer. By default, once
finished, the DVD will jump back to
the menu where the Track originated.

The last instruction is particularly important. You can manually choose where you
want the DVD to go, once that Track has finished playing.

Additional streams of audio can be added. Drag the audio from the Assets
window to any of the empty audio streams in the Track Editor. For
monitoring the Green buttons to the left can be toggled to switch between the
streams of audio.

One can then switch between audio streams when Simulating by pressing the
Audio symbol located to the left of the Simulator window.

Streams of Audio in the Track Editor

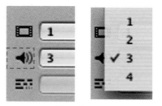

Simulator

When it comes to working with multiple streams of video you are dealing with a
more complex area.

If you are determined, and manage to get past all the technical hurdles,
be aware that multi-angles chew up loads of memory.

The Track Editor is not designed to be a full-featured editor. Rather it provides
the facility to perform simple editing functions such as trimming or arranging
clips, plus the ability to insert Chapter Markers, add Subtitles, and to arrange
multiple streams of audio.

Adding Markers Using the Track Editor

You may wish to use the Track Editor to enter Markers which can be used to build a Scene Index, jump from section to section, or to build Stories.

There are times when it is more efficient to enter Chapter Markers directly into the Track Editor, rather than going through the process inside of Final Cut. This is quick and easy to achieve.

There are two methods:

1 Click in the gray area above the incremental display in the Track Editor. A Chapter Marker will then be added.

Click to Add Chapter Markers

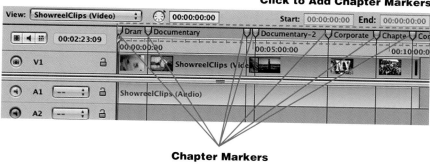

Chapter Markers

2 Alternatively, press the letter M twice. The added Chapter Marker can then be named in the Inspector.

To delete a Chapter Marker control-click on the Marker and select Delete Marker.

You can also choose to Simulate from a Marker which will Simulate the Track from that exact point.

THE FOCAL EASY GUIDE TO DVD STUDIO PRO 3

Stories

I think of Stories as being like a music CD. You can program the music tracks in any order. The difference being, with DVD Stories, that you get to program Video, Audio, and Graphics.

Stories let you play the contents of a Track in a different order to how the original Track was programmed to play. The beauty of using Stories is that this reordering of content does not consume any additional space on the DVD.

Stories work by playing Track Markers in a different order.

When building a Story you do not have to include all the markers which make up a track. You can be selective.

Stories could be used to modify a movie so that it is suitable for younger audience. A short version of a longer piece could be played as a teaser or promo material.

Chapters can also be duplicated, all without consuming any additional space on the DVD.

Each time you refer to the original Track, through Stories, no more room is consumed.

You can create up to 98 stories to play back track segments in any order you wish.

In the case of the project I am creating, which is my Showreel, I will step back to the preparation stage to produce a single track from which the stories will be based. The method I used earlier with the Track Editor was not very efficient.

In Final Cut Pro I created an end-to-end version of my Showreel featuring six individual clips. These are all edited together in one continuous Timeline and this is then exported as a Reference Movie and imported into DVD Studio Pro.

The Track Markers can be added either in Final Cut or DVD Studio Pro using the methods already described:

1   Drag the Track from the Assets window into the Menu Editor and connect it to a Button. In the case of the DVD being built I have already added the background and a button titled Play All.

Notice the Track now appears in the Outline View.

Click the Track in Outline View and it will now appear in the Track Editor.

2   If the Chapter Markers have not already been added then this needs to be done now.

Click in the gray area above the track itself or press the letter M twice.

It is important to get the Chapter Markers right as they will define the start of each Chapter within the Story.

1   Highlight the track you are working with in Outline View.

2   Click the icon at the top of the Toolbar titled **Add Story**. Beneath the Track you highlighted in the Outline window will appear the Story, titled Story 1.

Add Story

3   Highlight the Story in the Outline window.

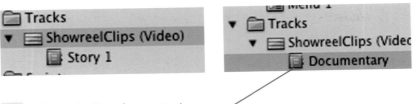

4   Name the Story by overtyping.

5   Double-click the renamed Story in Outline View and look to the Track Editor. You will see a window displaying the Markers of the Track as a list. The Markers listed on the left represent the original order of the markers within the Track. The window on the right, currently empty, is used to create the new order which the Track will play.

Track	Slideshow	Story	Script			
View: Documentary			⇕	ShowreelClips (Video)		
No.	Track	Duration	No.	Story	Running Time	
1	Start	00:00:0!				
2	Drama	00:01:0!				
3	Docume	00:02:0!				
4	Music	00:01:5!				
5	Docume	00:02:3!				
6	Corpora	00:03:0!				
7	Corpora	00:00:1!				

Original Track Order   New Track Order – currently empty

Outline	Story					
View:	Documentary		⋮	ShowreelClips (Video)		

No.	Track	Duration	No.	Story	Running Time
1	Start	00:00:0	1	Music	00:01:57:02
2	Drama	00:01:0	2	Document	00:03:58:13
3	Docume	00:02:0	3	Drama	00:05:01:06
4	Music	00:01:5	4	Corporate	00:08:08:04
5	Docume	00:02:3	5	Document	00:10:48:03
6	Corpora	00:03:0	6	Corporate	00:11:05:06
7	Corpora	00:00:1			

Original Track Order   New Track Order

Notice above that not only have the sections defined by Markers been reordered – I have only chosen to use six of the original seven.

6 To move sections from left to right in the Story window is as simple as picking up and dragging.

No.	Story	Running
1	Music	00:01:5
2	Document	00:03:5
3	Drama	00:05:0
45	Corporatent	00⦚08⦚⦚
5	Document	00:10:4
6	Corporate	00:11:0

7 Once positioned items can be reordered within the list by dragging up or down.

8 Press the Outline button to return to the overview of your DVD. Pick up the Story and drag it into the Menu Editor. Wait for the Drop Palette to appear.

9 Choose **Create Button. Connect to Story**. What you have done is created a Button which connects to the Story you have just built. This Story refers to the Track which is connected to the Play All button.

What I have decided to do is to create six individual Stories, each of which will connect to a button as per the original design of the DVD.

Each of the buttons will then play a Story which refers to the same Track as the Play All button.

Remember, the huge advantage of using Stories is there is no doubling up of the data used. The same Track is played in a different order with the markers serving as sign posts as to how the Track is played.

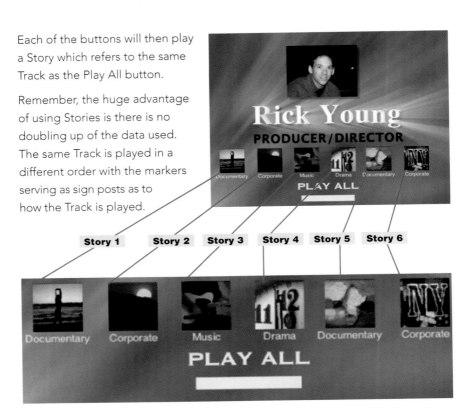

The Play All button, above, connects to the track which each of the six Stories refer to. Understand the concept and you are more than half-way home. At all times one needs to avoid doubling up of Video material. As soon as content is added to the available space on a DVD quickly fills up.

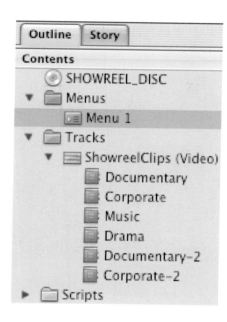

The image to the left shows the six separate stories listed. Each of these play the same track as the Play All button, the only difference being the order in which the track is played.

Within the structure of my Showreel I have chosen for each Story to play a single section of video. It would have been just as easy to have had different sections of video jump from one section within the track to another section. Working with Stories presents an immense amount of flexibility as to how the DVD can be structured, without the limitations of having to encode material at a low bit rate, necessarily, just to fit the material onto the DVD.

Track	Slideshow	Story	Script

View: Music ⧉   ShowreelClips (Video)

No.	Track	Duration		No.	Story Markers
1	Chapter 1	00:02:04:20		1	Music Entry
2	Documentar	00:03:42:06			
3	Corporate	00:04:00:12		For this story there is only	
4	Music	00:04:27:09		one item to be played.	
5	Drama	00:03:33:15			
6	Documentar	00:02:58:02			
7	Corporate-2	00:03:15:23			

The procedure in a few simple steps is as follows: add a Story, double-click the Story, drag the section or sections you need to build the Story, and connect the Story to a button by dragging from Outline View.

This is as far as I will go with investigating stories. It isn't necessary to show the construction of each of the six Stories as the procedure follows that which has been already demonstrated.

Converting a Slideshow into a Track

A useful function that can be performed in the Track Editor is to Convert a Slideshow to a Track.

This is incredibly simple to achieve:

1   To make a Slideshow active double-click the icon in Outline View, or double-click a Slideshow button in the Menu Editor. The familiar Slideshow controls will appear. Feel free to juggle the order of slides, change the duration, and add audio.

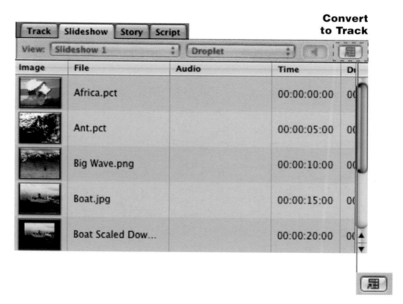

2   Once you are happy with the Slideshow press Convert to Track.

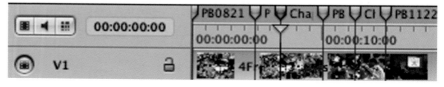

The Slideshow will then appear in the Track Editor, as a Track, with Chapter points separating each of the Slides.

The usefulness of this function is that once your Slideshow has been converted to a Track you can then add multiple Audio or Video streams, Subtitles, or achieve anything else that you can do with a track.

If you were to click a button which was previously connected to the Slideshow it will now connect to the Track which your Slideshow has been converted into.

You can undo the Convert to Track command by pressing Apple Z.

Subtitles

Many professional DVDs feature Subtitles. These are essential for many international releases and are not difficult to implement within your DVD structure.

1   Click twice in any of the Subtitle tracks to create a Subtitle.

2   Click the yellow area that appears in the Track Editor.

3   Type the Subtitle information directly into either the Menu Editor or the Text area in the Inspector.

4 Use the controls in the Inspector to program in fades and to adjust formatting. Exact positioning with regards to timing can also be adjusted. _____

5 Drag the ends of the Subtitles in the Timeline to extend or reduce the duration.

6 The color settings for Text, Outline, and Background can also be altered in the color settings in the Inspector.

For reference purposes the following color schemes apply to streams in the Track Editor.

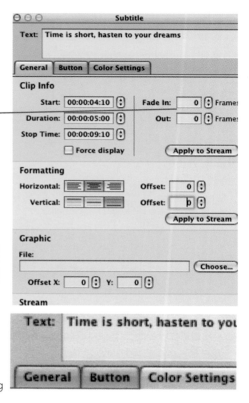

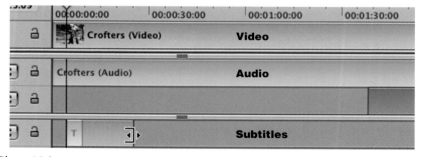

Blue – Video

Green – Audio

Yellow – Subtitles

Subtitles can be accessed when Simulating by toggling on and off the Subtitle Select button. Here you can switch between the Subtitle streams.

Subtitle Select

Drop down display enables you to switch between Subtitle Streams

Make sure the box titled View is checked

When playing back a DVD in a set-top player Subtitles are switched on and off using the remote control.

Working in the Track Editor is very different to working in the Timeline in Final Cut. You cannot apply effects, adjust levels or even perform overwrite edits. But for the quick reordering of content, adding multiple streams of Video, Audio or Subtitles, or to delve into the world of Stories, then the Track Editor is an area that needs to be investigated.

Basic Mode is fine for simple work but to take the knowledge further you must step into Advanced. Otherwise, you are limiting yourself to a fraction of what DVD Studio Pro has to offer.

Finishing Touches

The Showreel is looking good but there are a couple of tricks remaining to make it complete.

First, I want to include my CV so that a client has all of my details to look over. This will be included as data, in the form of DVD-ROM data. A DVD-ROM is like a big CD-ROM disk. For example, I could also choose to include other data such as still images.

Second, I want the viewer to be able to link direct to my website through what is known as DVD@ccess.

When I first delved into DVD authoring I was adamant that all I wanted to do was make DVD disks that looked professional. Really there wasn't any reason to worry about DVD-ROM content or linking to the web. That was a bit too technical and "out there" for me to want to deal with.

Then one day a client asked for both: DVD-ROM content and DVD Access. Standing tall I learnt how to do both. And it's not that hard.

Adding DVD-ROM Content

Once your DVD is authored for Video playback on set-top machines you might wish to include files as data which can be accessed when the disk is in a computer:

1   Click the icon representing your disk located at the top of the Outline window. Look to the Inspector.

2   Check the Content Box.

3   Press choose.

4 Navigate to a folder which is home to the material you wish to include. It is not possible to include data as individual documents – folders must be accessed to include data content.

5 Choose the folder.

If you get lost at any point make sure you have pressed the General tab of the Inspector. Alternatively, double-click the Disk icon at the top of Outline View.

The information displayed in the Inspector confirms the file(s) you have added and the path taken to access these.

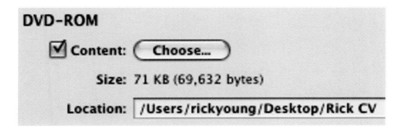

6 Check Joliet Extension support to confirm compatibility with the file name structure on the PC platform.

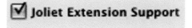

Once you have burnt your disk you can then access the data files by inserting the DVD into a computer; close the DVD Player if one opens; double-click the DVD icon on the desktop and access the documents inside of the named folder.

Adding DVD Access

This refers to getting the DVD to link to a website when the DVD is playing in an Internet–connected computer. This is surprisingly easy to achieve.

The first thing you need to understand is that this will be accessed when the DVD is playing, unlike DVD-ROM data which is accessed when the DVD Player is closed.

The method I have used is to set the DVD so that the command to link to the website is invoked when you press a button which links to a menu. Therefore, you need to create a Menu as a home place for the DVD Access command plus you also need to create a button on this menu so the viewer can then return to the home menu (or whatever options you choose to include).

1   Press Add Menu.

Add Menu

2   Look to the Inspector which will now display details regarding the Menu. Click Advanced, the Fifth tab at the top of the Menu.

3   Check the DVD@ccess box.

4   Enter a name.

5   Enter a web address including the http://information. This is important.

6   Include a button on the Main menu of your DVD and target this to the menu just created. When the viewer presses this button, assuming they are in a computer connected to the web, they will then be connected to the Menu which takes them to the web address you have entered.

7   On the Menu created for DVD@ccess you need to create another button so the viewer can return to the Home menu or wherever you choose.

The Graphical View

The best way to understand what the Graphical View does is to observe it throughout the process of building DVDs. When you add a Menu, Track, Story, or Slideshow an additional tile is added to the Graphical View. This represents the new item which has been added to the DVD.

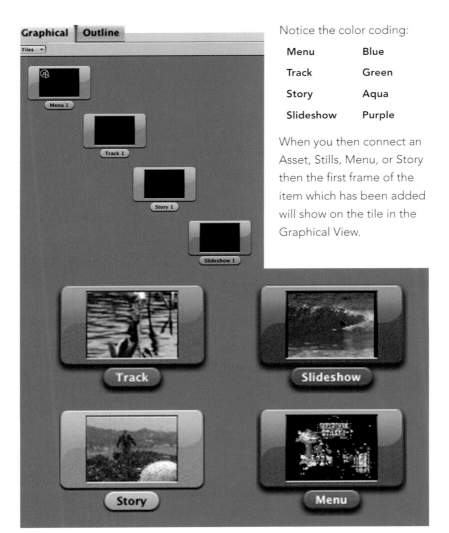

Notice the color coding:

Menu	Blue
Track	Green
Story	Aqua
Slideshow	Purple

When you then connect an Asset, Stills, Menu, or Story then the first frame of the item which has been added will show on the tile in the Graphical View.

Menus, Tracks, Stories, and Slideshows can be deleted using the Graphical View. The space consumed by those assets will then be reclaimed. This provides a quick and easy alternative than jumping into the Outline window. To delete, highlight any of the items in the Graphical View and press the delete key. Nice and easy!

Control-click on any of the tiles and a series of options will appear.

Several of these are quite useful:

First Play – provides the ability to set the first play of the DVD to any Menu, Track, Slideshow, or Story. An icon representing a DVD will then appear on the tile which has been set to be the first play.

Choose add and a contextual menu will appear giving you the ability to create addition Menus, Tracks, and Slideshows.

Zoom to selection centers the Graphical View so you can focus on a particular area you are working with.

FlagTile – I think of this as a bit like adding a marker in Final Cut Pro. It points out that there is something important regarding this tile.

Delete – Gets rid of the tile, be in Menu, Track, Slideshow or Story, and any assets connected to it. The space consumed by these assets will be reclaimed.

Duplicate – Creates a copy of a tile and any assets connected with it. This will add to the space being consumed on your DVD.

Simulate – Lets you Simulate from a specific tile, be it a Track, Slideshow, Story, or Menu. This can be much easier than going to the Simulator and viewing the disk from the very beginning. Simulating from within the Graphical View lets you immediately Simulate from a chosen point.

The size of the Graphical View can be expanded and contracted in size.
By dragging the bars at the edges of the window or by clicking the controls at the top. Just as the Timeline can be contracted and expanded in Final Cut so the apparent size of the Graphical View can also be contracted and expanded.

You can also resize the Graphical window by positioning your cursor at the edge of the window – your cursor will change to two vertical lines with arrows at the center. Drag and the window will be resized.

Note: If you select all (Apple+A) you can then move all the tiles together.

If you find that you are getting into a bit of a mess with the Graphical View choose the Arrange Menu and scroll to Distribute Objects. Then choose Autolayout and everything will be neatly put into position and scaled to the overall size of the Graphical window.

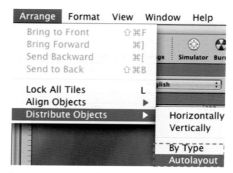

Alternatively choose by **By Type** for an alternative view of the structure of your DVD.

Note the controls at top of the interface.

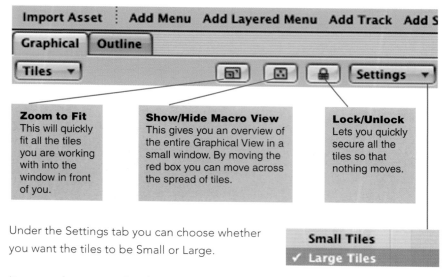

Under the Settings tab you can choose whether you want the tiles to be Small or Large.

Items can be renamed in the Graphical View. Double-click directly onto the name of a Tile and then retype as you wish.

Note: The renaming of tiles will have the effect of renaming items in Outline View.

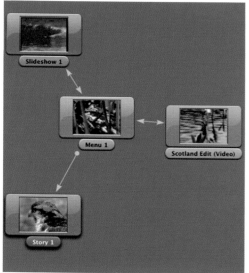

The Lines between each of the tiles are called Connection Lines. These show which elements are connected and the arrows on the ends show what is being targeted.

The Graphical View gives you an overview of the structure of your DVD. You can quickly spot items which are not in use and easily delete them or decide a strategy of how to deal with them.

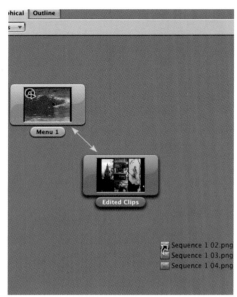

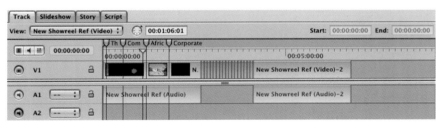

A great little trick is to edit content together by dragging Assets direct from the Asset window onto a track tile – these are green. Drop tracks or slides and automatically the items will be arranged sequentially. This can be then viewed in the Track Editor which shows the track you have built.

If you were to drag Assets from the Assets window into the

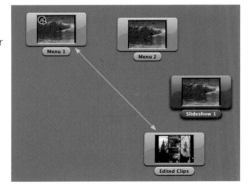

Graphical View and release these in the gray area, you can then create Tracks and Slideshows. These will then need to be connected to buttons so they will work within the structure of your disk. When working in Advanced Mode this is achieved by dragging items from within the Outline window to the Menu Editor.

As would be expected, either of these methods will add content to your disk.

Do not be afraid in any way of the Graphical View. It is there to make your life easier. Just keep an eye on it while you work and you'll quickly get the hang of what it does and how to use it.

Transitions

Transitions provide a way to spruce up your DVD and to give it a level of sophistication. Many jobs in editing may effects heavy; so it is with DVDs. Some clients just love to have their production sparkle. When this is the requirement turn to the transitions.

Transitions can be used when going from a menu into a track, a menu into a Slideshow, a menu to a menu, or within a Slideshow itself. Transitions can also be used between each of the individual slides.

The word transition, by definition, means to progress; transform; metamorphosis; to go from one state into another.

So it is with video. The moving image goes from one form into another with the transition providing the visual transformation.

Standard and Alpha Transitions

There are two types of transitions: **standard** and **alpha**.

1. In the Menu Editor click a button and look to the Inspector.

2. Click the fourth Tab along, titled Transition. You now have access to the transition controls and a drop-down menu from which each of the transitions can be chosen.

3 Click the drop-down menu and this will reveal all the transitions you have to work with.

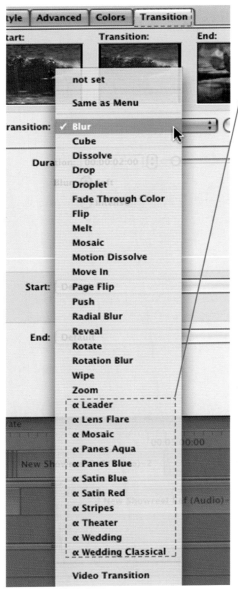

The **standard** transitions are listed from the top of the list to just over half-way down. Beyond this, denoted by a fish-like symbol, are the **alpha** transitions. You can choose standard or alpha just by clicking from within the list.

The difference between standard and alpha transitions is obvious when you see the result. For a quick idea of what to expect choose a transition and press the preview button.

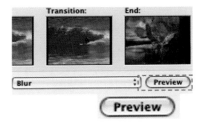

The standard transitions simply effects from one Video source to another, while the alpha transitions actually use the video as a part of the effect itself.

The way the standard transition works is the out-going shot will freeze and then transition to a freeze of the in-coming shot. The transition happens at the center point between the freezes.

Alpha transitions are visually different. The out-going and in-coming shots still freeze, however the look is more animated or effects based. Try each of the transitions to see the result.

DVD Studio Pro builds the transitions for you. You can modify timing and the direction of the transition.

Transitions can be applied to buttons connecting to tracks, between slides which make up a Slideshow, or from menu to menu.

As enticing as transitions may be it is worth using them sparingly – the "less is more" rule applies.

While they may add sparkle and posaz to getting from one part of the DVD to another, the transition is secondary to the content the viewer is about to watch.

Working with Transitions

Make sure you have a background set in the Menu Editor and a button with a track connected to it. Make sure the track which is connected does not start in black:

1   Click the button and look to the Inspector.

2   Click the Fourth tab along – Transitions.

3   Click the Transition Drop-Down menu. These are the choices you have to work with.

4   Press the Preview button to see the result.

5 Choose the Simulator and press the button to see the transition properly.

6 Close the Inspector and choose another transition if you wish.

One can easily alter the duration and transition type for both standard and alpha transitions. Different controls are provided in the Inspector depending on which transition is chosen.

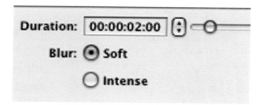

To be clear about what the Transition window is showing here are the details.

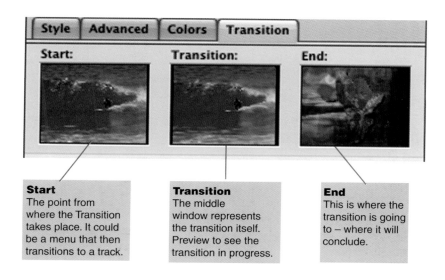

Start
The point from where the Transition takes place. It could be a menu that then transitions to a track.

Transition
The middle window represents the transition itself. Preview to see the transition in progress.

End
This is where the transition is going to – where it will conclude.

Experiment with transitions. Some quite nice effects can be achieved.

Transitions with Slideshows

When building Slideshows transitions can be programmed for individual slides or as a global command – meaning the transition will apply to all.

To apply a transition to all the slides in a Slideshow simply open the Transition tab at the top of the Slideshow Editor and select the type of transition. By default this is set to "No Transition". Once you have selected a transition it will apply to all the slides in the Slideshow.

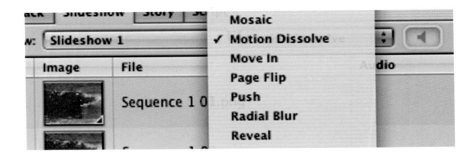

To change the transition for individual slides make sure the Transition command is set to **No Transition** in the Slideshow Editor.

Click a slide and then choose the transition type from the controls in the Inspector.

Once a Transition is set a triangle will appear at the bottom right of the slides icon.

The Inspector is where you can set transitions for individual slides. Different sets of controls are available depending on which transition has been chosen.

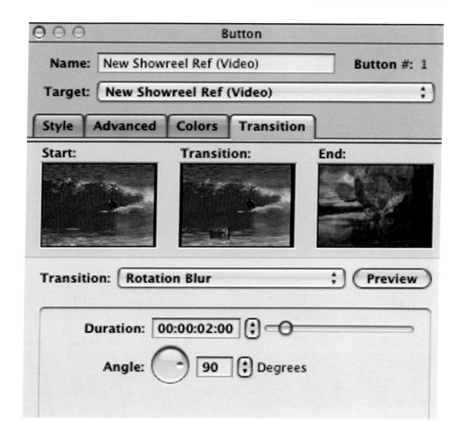

I kept the Graphical View and Transition until last for the simple reason that you can comfortably ignore them and get on with DVD authoring process without delving into these areas at all.

In DVD Studio Pro 2 there was no Graphical View and there were no transitions to experiment with.

Use the Graphical View to make sure all the pieces that make up your DVD are in place as they should be.

Use Transitions with care. Some are subtle, others jarring.

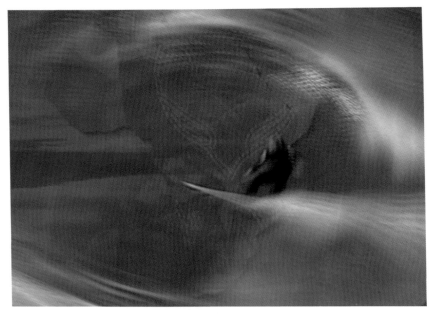

Standard Transitions in action

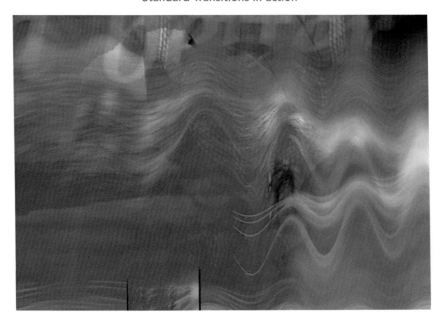

Standard Transitions in action

Alpha Transitions in action

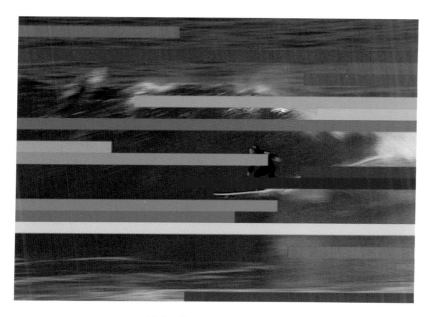

Alpha Transitions in action

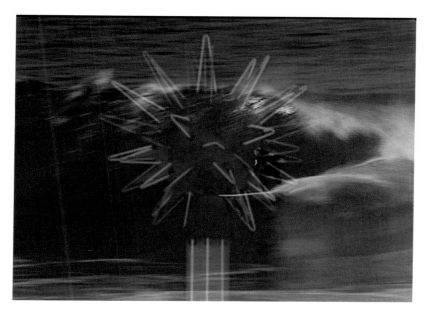

CHAPTER 15
TIME MACHINE

The Future

Tape is going to go away.

A lot more is going to be done in ram.

We'll all be able to access high speed internet
from anywhere on the planet with a device no
bigger than a credit card.

And the world will keep on turning to the
beat of the silicon chip.

My prediction is that Apple's suite of authoring tools
will be everywhere. In schools and offices, peoples homes
and production facilities for all types of media.

Sure there will be competing products;
high end; low end; PC and everything in between.

But for those who want the best without spending
fifty or a hundred thousand dollars, pounds or Euro's,
then it's Final Cut and DVD Studio Pro all the way.

Because we can afford it, because it works and because, for
the money, it's streets ahead of anything else out there.

CHAPTER 16
WORDS FROM THE MASTERS

Jonathan Smiles, Managing Director, Digital Safari Limited

www.digitalsafari.net

Clients: Apple Computer, Microsoft, BSkyB, Shell, and 20th Century Fox.

A client comes to you with a project – what is the very first thing you do – obviously you've got to talk to the client, find out the requirements. What are the thought processes you go through and what questions do you put forward?

Well the question that comes out depends on what they're making. Does the material already exist? Do we have to shoot any new material or are we talking about a totally new production. Then we're into looking at where it is going to be released, is it European or is it going to be a worldwide release? We may look about into the US side of things, what are our timescales, what are our deadlines. From all that you can work out what it is going to cost them.

Once you've got an idea of those crucial things that you have just outlined, what are the processes that you go through in your mind.

Number one is running time – how much material we're going to try and put on the disks. We need to know whether it's going to be a single or dual layer production, or whether it is going to be multiple disks. We need to be fully aware of any implications such as surround audio being mixed. Is it Menu design?

Now – it's been said to me before that a DVD is only as good as its menus – so how crucial in the whole scheme of the DVD is the actual look, and the feel and the shape of the menus.

Most DVD authors get way overstressed about menus. The people watching the material are interested in the content itself and menus are merely a way of finding it. So you can find there's a lot of productions where the menus just take over, and menus should give you the look and feel but they should in no way hinder your access to the material.

Having said that do you think the idea of keeping things simple on the DVD is a good strategy?

Yes! It's got to be so that your grandmother can use the disk. So basically they want to watch the movie or they may want to watch the extras. They don't want to have the superduper animated menu making them wait for 10 minutes before they can watch the feature. So there's some very basic interactivity rules you need to apply; that is, they need to be able to get into the content quickly.

So for a disk to be effective it doesn't have to be a technical masterpiece.

Yes! The disk is purely about delivering the content.

What would be your advice to someone who is new to DVD authoring?

Think of the menus linking together linear pieces of video. Think about how somebody will actually watch it – are they going to watch the movie or do this. Have something that simplifies things so if there are lots of options can they just have an option that says "Play All". And as such you have to be much aware if you're doing international projects that English may not be their first language so you may need to make things more internationally friendly.

Is there a general formula that you would work to when putting together DVDs. For example, Main Movie, Slideshow, and Additional Material.

Well for Hollywood movies there is definitely – each studio has its way of how it has its movies presented. So you always see sort of Play Movies, Scene Selection, Setup or Languages, and Extras. And they'll be pretty much mandated from the top. For the music titles I work with you are normally, working with the band or artist themselves and some of the personalities of them will come through. And sometimes you can take more liberties with a music production, something like Visions of the Beast by Iron Maiden, which has very very intricate 3D menus, but it's very much in keeping with the Iron Maiden style.

But generally for a Hollywood movie you would expect it to work the same way.

It seems to me with the Templates you can very easily throw just your material into it and then customize them to your own needs as well.

Yep! Or you can make your own Templates. So there's a lot of production companies that will do all their Rushes and Showreels, and have a template which they use and that's what they work with.

Where do you see DVD authoring going over the next 5–10 years?

DVD itself in the medium term is going to get replaced – there's going to be a High Definition version turning up. The DVD format at the moment is very much the same as it was in 1996 when it was released. So nothing has really changed. Except the tools have come down in price from being sort of a million dollars to get into DVD authoring down to the price of your Mac. And stick a Decklink card in there to do standard definition and you can do pretty much anything. So it's very much wide open.

What is most important – understanding the technical side of DVD authoring or understanding creatively how to make it look good and making everything easy to access?

I would say making it look good and good interaction. The technology – you don't need to know the DVD video specification anymore. DVD Studio Pro has totally simplified it and you can just get on and make it. So it's back down to straightforward design talent.

Would you agree what you need to know technically will become second nature after you have made a few disks? The important part is the creative thought processes that go into authoring the disk.

Within reason. There are still some cases where you still have to have technical knowledge to design things properly. But in general most of the things are taken care of for you. You've got things as easy as iDVD to use without being able to customize it to the nth degree and having all the professional features like multi-angles and multiple languages, and all those things.

What other applications would you use?

Most of them are down to designing graphics. Final Cut to do the video, might use After Effects, Photoshop, or Combustion to create the menu elements. You can do a lot of stuff within DVD Studio Pro but you'd still probably end up using Photoshop, After Effects, and Combustion to do some of your animations and things. And these will be the things that will normally set apart one DVD author from another.

Just tell me a bit about using a hardware card for encoding. What is the advantage of this?

Yeah – I use Media Press Pro SDI. It is real time. You can see the compression as it goes through and if you're talking about a lot of longer material that's coming off existing tapes, off Digi-Betas, you go straight from SDI to compressed, and then drop that straight into the DVD and make it. You don't have this extra compression step. It will work with files from within Final Cut – you can put them through the card – but it's not as fast when you do it that way. But I have a cheat where I use two machines. I have a Final Cut machine connected to another machine running the encoder so you literally just play them across SDI in real time. It becomes very important for things like the Times – the first DVDs which I worked on where we had very little time to make them. Tapes were turning up at the last moment and then to be able to do it in real time becomes indispensable. With a G5 now you're getting very close to real time at the lower qualities and at the maximum quality about one-and-a-half to two times real time. So we could do it on a G5 but the hardware option gives you that extra margin – the comfort of being able to do things quickly.

Any final comment?

DVDs are ubiquitous now. Standalone DVD Recorders are now affordable for consumers. Recordable DVDs are everywhere. It has basically taken over. I've been making DVDs since 1997.

John Pin, Managing Director, DVD'z, Sydney, Australia
jpin@optushome.com.au

Clients: Columbia Tri-star, 21st Century Pictures, Timelife, and Shock Records.

A client comes to you with a job, they approach you, what sort of questions do you ask, how do you approach the job?

I first try to get an overall sense of the project. Is it a movie, animation, or documentary? In what format are the vision and audio masters? Is it stereo or surround. How much freedom do I have in the design? Does the client have any specific requests about structure. So, I'm basically trying to get an overview of the title and to determine how much direction from the client there will be.

Once you've got some sort of an idea of what the client requires, what sort of processes go through your mind practically as you go through the authoring process.

Once I have the job I map it out. A lot of this will depend on if there has been any specific direction that I need to adhere to or if I have been given freedom to what to approach the title as I see fit. If someone comes to me with basically a story book or the whole thing mapped out saying we want this menu opening up to these menus then I work to that. But you see a lot of the time my clients don't come to me with any instruction. In fact just about all my clients give me no instruction and I'm just expected to produce titles that are to budget. The majority of my clients are independents who do not have huge budgets to throw at their DVD releases. These companies have licensed a project and they want their product out economically – yet looking fantastic. They know my work and will trust my judgement.

Do they give you a budget to work to?

They know my price. It will vary depending on the title. I have a standard price that I do for a "Vanilla" title. That would be a movie feature with a trailer or two.

This price would then vary if the audio was surround. As time is money in business, anything that requires more time will cause the price to go up.

My clients know my price and that of course will be their budget most of the time. However, they might come to me with a project that they wish to do a little more with. Perhaps they have a director's commentary or maybe they would like to produce one. This would all be costed and worked into an overall budget.

And if it's a new client that I haven't worked with before I might go back to them and say okay "I think this is what we are going to do. I think it would be great if we did this or that … discuss the budget. Once this is in place I will then go about the process of preparing assets and authoring".

Is their a general formula which you work to – it seems to me, certainly with Hollywood releases, you've got your Main Movie, Additional Material, Subtitles, and Scene Index. Is it formulaic or is it not?

Absolutely. Ninety percent of the work that I do is very similar. I mentioned before about "Vanilla" titles. Well, they are basically all the same in their construction. Of course they don't have the same menus, but they all have a Title menu, and they all have Chapter menus. There is uniformity in their design. If you take out the DVDs you have in your home and study their structure you will notice, if you haven't already, standard structures. It is exactly what you're saying. There will generally be some type of Copyright Notice or Warning Declaration at the front; then there'll be a Main Movie and then there may be additional material – perhaps a trailer or a few interviews. There is always a Main menu and Submenus, such as Chapter menus, or perhaps an Extra Features menu.

You will see a lot of biographies and filmographies. It is inexpensive to add such content. And in the thoughts of many clients they feel they are adding value.

Yes, structurally, many more DVDs will have similarities. It is seldom that you get someone who comes to you with something outside of that. It does happen of course. But most of the time it will be another piece of footage. So, it is really just another bit of footage that will need a button on a menu somewhere. It is very rare that a client will come with an idea that will need scripting.

So would you agree "the keep it simple strategy" is a good one?

Absolutely! Never make things complicated. Always keep things simple. As simple as you can to get your job done. That's the heart of anything that's good, isn't it.

On the other hand, if you run a business you will want to make sure your work is of a high standard. You have to try and keep things interesting. You always have to keep a certain standard and you always look for opportunities to do something special or something nice. It doesn't have to be revolutionary, it might just be a few tasteful transitions to menus or perhaps a little something special in the compositing of a menu. You know, it's all about the visual, you know people see a DVD they see the menu. Clients see a DVD they see the menu. That's what they see.

So don't go and put all your work into other areas, like into writing amazing scripts that achieve little and neglect your menu design. You may have done a fabulous job on some interaction, but if the menu looks cheap … you've let yourself down.

What's in front of you on the screen when that DVD goes into a player is the first impression you give to the viewer. When it comes to the main everyone will notice if its not up to scratch. Your work will be judged on this I think.

Something I see on many DVDs that I think is not desirable are overly complicated menus. The big mistake sometimes is creating long animated menus that lock out the buttons for a period of time. If you are going to have transitions and animations leading to menus, remember that people will want to click through the DVD. If they have to wait, even just 3 or 4 seconds every time they hit a button for a transition to complete, they will get frustrated. Always think about the end user.

So more than anything make your menus look good and that will give your DVD the professional touch.

Absolutely. The menus have to look great … They've got to look professional. Put time into your menus. Even if you are doing a home DVD, remember the menu will sit on screen for extended periods of time.

Take a guess. Over the next 5–10 years what's going to happen with all these DVD authoring technologies. Where is it going?

I think DVD authoring technology – it will become just like word processing. I think it'll be accessible to everybody. With programs like DVD Studio Pro and Adobe Encore it is already opening up to millions of people. But eventually, as High Definition comes in I think this DVD specification will evolve into a newer format. It will be backward compatible of course. But new read/write technologies will arrive along with new media capable of holding far more information that we have now. It will open doors. Content will be written to take advantage of all these. It will evolve. I think web connectivity will come into its own over the next couple of years. That has been a stumbling block in the early years of DVD. I think we will see web interaction increasingly gain greater functionality. As this happens, content developers and content owners will want to take advantage of this.

What's your advice to the person who is new to all these technologies and is wondering how on earth they are ever going to even be able to make a disk.

I don't think you need to be familiar with every aspect of the technology to make DVDs. It is something you can learn as the need necessitates. If you're looking to take snapshots and home videos and turn them into DVDs, just have a go. You will find that it is not as difficult as you may think. There is no need to know what a GOP structure is or how to "bit budget". Many of the authoring packages have templates and, drag-and-drop environments that hide a lot of the technical stuff. Keeps it all in the background. Using these methods, you will create wonderful DVDs and commit to disk a lot of great moments.

Perhaps in time you may wish to explore, to break away from the Templates that a lot of programs provide you with. At this stage it will be time to learn a little bit more. But at first, certainly at a consumer level, have no fear. Just leap in. That's what I'd do.

What is important – understanding the technical side of things or getting the creative side together?

Well it depends what you want to do. You don't need to be able to build a car engine to be a good driver. So in DVD production if you're creative with some graphic design or creative with a DV camera and editing package, whatever you're using – be creative! Use the packages to bring that creativity together onto your DVD.

The technology is not necessarily there to be understood from A to Z. Just learn what you need to and progress from there.

Would you agree the technical side will become second nature as you become familiar with the application? The important stuff is the thought process that goes into the authoring itself.

As with a lot of things, DVD authoring can seem a bit daunting at first. But really there isn't that much to building a simple DVD at all. It's not rocket science and most of the program GUIs out there will hide a lot of the rocket science from you. And so just do it. Once you've done one or two you won't be overwhelmed by everything. It's pretty sequential. It's not difficult. And slowly you will learn the terminologies used in authoring and encoding. Yes I agree, by doing you will become increasingly aware of the technical side of things.

What other applications do you use?

We use Adobe After Effects, Photoshop, and we use a suite of imaging tools, mainly Adobe. After Effects is the main compositor. We started authoring with DVD Maestro in 1999. This was a fantastic program that revolutionized the DVD industry back then. As you know, Apple bought Spruce and Maestro. This is why I have kept a close eye on the development of DVD Studio Pro. I believe Apple retained a lot of Spruce engineers to assist in the revamping of DVD Studio Pro that has now come to fruition.

From what you have seen of DVD Studio Pro how good is it and what impact is it having on the market at both consumer and professional levels?

Well the first incarnation of DVD Studio Pro didn't impress me. It was limited and the encoder that was packaged with it needed development. Since I kept a close eye on it.

Now the program has come of age. You can get excellent encoding results and the authoring package is intuitive and powerful. It's a very sleek package.

Yes I believe DVD Studio Pro is shaking the authoring industry. In fact I know it is. It makes authoring easy, it removes the technical obstacles, and allows people's creativity to flow.

Jeff Warmouth
Author – DVD Authoring with DVD Studio Pro 2
(published by Focal Press).
Assistant Professor Communications Media Department,
Fitchberg State College, MA, USA
Has independently authored many DVDs through his
company Media Manic
www.mediamanic.tv

What's the first thing you do when someone comes to you and says they want to make a DVD? What sort of questions do you ask?

The thing I start asking them is what the scope of the project is. How much video they are going to have. How they want the structure to be, or, in other words, how they want to create an experience for the user. If they have thought about what the menus should look like or have they thought about any of that stuff. Sometimes clients have considered these issues and sometimes they haven't. So it's really figuring out, trying to get a sense of what the scope and the structure of the project are going to be.

And once you have an idea of the scope and the structure what sort of processes go through your mind practically in terms of getting the authoring process together.

Really try to get a schedule and figure out what actual activities are going to have to happen. So, is there going to be some editing that happens beforehand. Or are they providing material that's completely ready to go. Are we going to have to build the menus – obviously we will build the menus but what's going to go into those menus do they want Motion menus, do they want menus that include material from the video that they're giving us.

But before doing anything, before doing any actual physical work, I really put together a detailed description of the project. A list of assets. So how much video and audio is there going to be and how this will be subdivided into pieces. So is there going to be eight separate video and audio pieces on the disk or eight separate tracks. So I get a really good solid list of all of the elements that are going to be used and then I put a flow chart together. That's a sort of a visual description of all of the elements that are going to go onto the DVD. From the first thing that the user's going to see, includes all of the choices that the user's going to make.

How rigid would you be regarding sticking to that flow chart?

I tend to be pretty flexible. A flow chart is really just a guideline so – actually, I find quite often, that the menus that I designed for my flow chart end up being a bit too complicated and we end up combining some menus. For example, with one project that I did – it was a Tai Chi DVD. It was an instructional DVD. One particular Tai Chi sequence has 113 separate movements, or 113 little pieces of the sequence. And the client wanted each one of those pieces to be selectable from a menu. Well how do you do that? You can't put 113 buttons on a menu. So then we had to figure out what's the least number of menus we can create so that it's relatively simple for the viewer to access all that information. So it's a sort of a juggling act. And we actually redid menus three or four times for that project because of the initial flow chart; it was just too many menus, just so many that it would be too complicated for the viewer to go through.

Would you agree "the keep it simple strategy" is a good one.

Oh yeah. I do. It's difficult, I mean I'm sort of torn on that issue because DVD Studio Pro gives you the creative freedom to make extremely complex DVDs, and very complex choices and menus that have all kinds of choices and all kinds of elements. But, you know at the end of the day if you're doing a project for a client and the real aim is the content; then you've really got to be careful about how you design the DVD. It's really about information design. How do you design the information in a way that is simple for people to walk through and I think that's part of the challenge of designing. How to keep it simple, yet elegant, and interesting. You know, how to make menus that are going to be compelling and interesting but ultimately don't get in the way of the users' experience of trying to watch the movie or the video content of whatever the DVD is. That's always the trick. And I think it varies from project to project. So if you're doing a DVD for a Hollywood movie then you've got to keep it really simple because people have just got to hit play and watch the movie. But let's say you're doing a two DVD set and one disk is the movie and the second disk is extras. Well that could be as wild as you want it to be, as it's the supplemental material.

It seems looking at Hollywood DVDs they all work to a formula: you've basically got a main menu; some sort of extras like the making of, the trailers whatever; and then you've got the scene breakdown. So how formulaic is DVD production?

That's a good one. I wouldn't say that production itself is formulaic but you're right there is certainly a formula for Hollywood DVDs. And that's a sort of unfortunate in that – I mean I see it with my students that they already seem to know what a DVD is. They know what's supposed to be on a DVD – right! You know there's a Main Movie, there's a Scene Selection, there's a making of documentary, there's a trailer, there's some cast and crew bios. That's a sort of the basic formula. But at the same time, even in Hollywood disks, I've seen some pretty interesting stuff. Some pretty innovative uses of DVD features like, for example, on the Moulin Rouge DVD there is a sort of a little extra segment where you can edit your own dance sequence from the dance numbers that they do in the film. It's a multi-angle little segment and you can switch back and forth between the different angles and essentially edit in quasi-real time, a dance number from four different camera angles. That's pretty interesting. It's quirky. It's not a particularly useful feature but it's fun and innovative use of the specification.

If you go outside the Hollywood formula you get some really interesting features that push the specification in, I think, really powerful ways.

There's a formula but I think people are trying to break it.

The other interesting, you know I would say, mainstream Hollywood push for DVDs to pull out of the formula is the Lord of the Rings DVD series, in which they released the theatrical – a version of the theatrical release – but then there's a brand new version of the film that's released strictly on DVD, later on in the four DVD set. And again I think that's another place where DVDs are being used outside of that very restrictive formula.

Where do you see DVD authoring going in the next 5–10 years?

I think the big thing that's going to turn everything on its head is High Definition. There are a bunch of people scrambling to figure out how to put High Definition onto DVD. There are three or four different specifications that they're arguing about, as usual. Hopefully they do come up with one standard, rather than three. But hopefully what'll happen once they do figure out a standard is to really build in some more complexity into the DVD specification itself. So that on those High Definition DVDs you could create maybe complex games that could run on a standard DVD Player that are part of the specification, part of the standard.

The problem really in predicting what's going to happen with authoring is that the DVD specification was laid down between 1995 and 1997 when the DVD forum was establishing the DVD specification. Once they locked that down it's unchanging. You can't change the specification. Right you can't change that standard so all these authoring systems, DVD Studio Pro included, even though they make the experience of authoring more innovative, or they make the process easier for the author – the specification hasn't changed.

I mean I think DVD Studio Pro itself is pretty dog-gone innovative in the way that it allows you to really work in a kind of what-you-see-is-what-you-get environment. In the way that you can build menus from different elements right there in the authoring system.

Where's it going to go from there? Besides High Definition I don't know if I can predict.

What's your advice to someone starting off with DVD Studio Pro and thinks where on earth do I begin?

Keep it simple.

I would say start with Basic Mode and add tools as you need them. DVD Studio Pro is really unique in that it allows you to build disks very very simple. This is pretty unprecedented in the authoring world.

I would say start simple. Keep it simple then add the advanced stuff only as you need it.

That's it in a nutshell.

What is most important – understanding the technical side of what DVD authoring is about or the creative requirements. Is it more important to understand the technical stuff or the creative side?

I would say it's a balance but absolutely the creative side is important. An innovative Menu can really make or break the disk. Make or break the impact that your disk has on its audience. But in terms of technical issues about menu design in itself, really important things such as staying within the Title Safe Area, I think that is very important. I think that can make or break someone seeing your disk as professional or not. Using fonts that work well on the television. And good composition. Good design and composition of the menus is very important.

The same kind of issues you would think of if you were designing something for the page. Or like an intro. graphic sequence, good balance between the elements on the screen. But also making sure that – I guess, rather, balancing visual design with ease of use. I think that's the real challenge with DVD menu design. Making them look good but also having them be simple for the user to access.

And designing so that they can easily use the very limited controls of the remote control. The DVD remote control is not a mouse you have up, down, left, right, and okay buttons. Right. So I think designing within that limited control set is very important as well.

What other applications do you use in the authoring process?

Photoshop and Final Cut Pro. I use Omnigraffle for making flow charts, Apple DVD Player for testing DVDs, and After Effects for designing motion content.

And when I'm working with any Subtitle content then I use Excel pretty heavily.

PCs vs Mac? Any comment?

That's a really interesting question actually because DVD Studio Pro is based on Spruce DVD Maestro which Apple bought. And that was originally Windows NT. Spruce runs on Windows NT and you can still find copies of Spruce around, and there are still people using Spruce. It's very stable.

One of the great things about Mac is that it's not a business-computing machine so they're designed to be video systems from the ground up. And that makes them a real pleasure to work on.

Index

Focal Press

www.focalpress.com

Join Focal Press online

As a member you will enjoy the following benefits:

- browse our full list of books available
- view sample chapters
- order securely online

Focal eNews

Register for eNews, the regular email service from Focal Press, to receive:

- advance news of our latest publications
- exclusive articles written by our authors
- related event information
- free sample chapters
- information about special offers

Go to www.focalpress.com to register and the eNews bulletin will soon be arriving on your desktop!

If you require any further information about the eNews or www.focalpress.com please contact:

USA
Tricia Geswell
Email: t.geswell@elsevier.com
Tel: +1 781 313 4739

Europe and rest of world
Lucy Lomas-Walker
Email: l.lomas@elsevier.com
Tel: +44 (0) 1865 314438

Catalogue

For information on all Focal Press titles, our full catalogue is available online at www.focalpress.com, alternatively you can contact us for a free printed version:

USA
Email: c.degon@elsevier.com
Tel: +1 781 313 4721

Europe and rest of world
Email: j.blackford@elsevier.com
Tel: +44 (0) 1865 314220

Potential authors

If you have an idea for a book, please get in touch:

USA
editors@focalpress.com

Europe and rest of world
ge.kennedy@elsevier.com

The Focal Easy Guide to Final Cut Pro 4

Rick Young

"Short, clear and to the point ... It will get you up and running on FCP in short order."
Ken Stone (www.kenstone.net), Los Angeles FCP user group

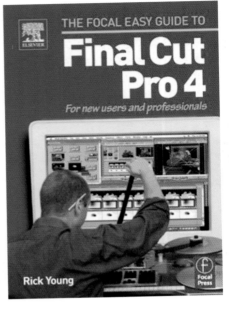

1 Save time, learn all you need to know to edit professionally with FCP4 fast!

2 Concise color coverage, written for FCP4 but relevant to all versions

3 Unique coverage of the new power of Soundtrack and LiveType, now free with FCP4

In this highly visual, color book, Rick Young covers all the essential areas: the interface, set-up and capture, editing, rendering, effects, audio and output, as well as a unique, invaluable introduction to the power of LiveType, Compressor and Soundtrack (these applications are also included with Final Cut Pro 4).

With this book you can start cutting immediately, whatever you edit, whatever the format. This is an ideal introduction whether you are a professional moving over to Final Cut Pro from another package or system, a new user, or a real-world film maker who wants to get the best results from Final Cut Pro, fast!

ISBN: 0 240 51925 6

For more details and to purchase a copy online visit **www.focalpress.com**